A
Beautiful
Patience

40
Life Lessons from Sūrah Yūsuf

SHABBIR HASSAN

Imam Ghazali PUBLISHING

Contents

Fa-ṣabrun jamīl
The profound statement of
'A Beautiful Patience' as mentioned by
Prophet Yaʿqūb ﷺ, the father of Yūsuf ﷺ
in verses 18 and 83 of Sūrah Yūsuf.

Dedication

To my beloved wife,
whose love keeps me nourished.
To my beautiful parents,
whose prayers allow me to flourish.

A Beautiful Patience

First published in Great Britain by Shabbir Hassan, 2021.

First Edition August 2021.

International Edition March 2023.

ISBN: 978-1-3999-0095-9 (Casebound)

978-1-952306-41-9 (International Paperback)

Cover design, illustration and typesetting: Jannah Haque.

Editing: Anna Birawi.

For bulk orders and wholesale, please contact the distributor of Imam Ghazali Publishing: Sattaur Publishing at info@sattaurpublishing.com or www.sattaurpublishing.com.

Transliteration Key

Arabic consonants

ء	ʾ	ض	ḍ
ث	th	ط	ṭ
ح	ḥ	ظ	ẓ
د	d	ع	ʿ
ذ	dh	ق	q
س	s	ك	k
ش	sh	ه	h
ص	ṣ		

Long vowels

ـَا	ā
ـِي	ī
ـُو	ū

Dipthongs

ـَوْ	aw
ـَيْ	ay

Chapter Dedications

The chapters of this book are dedicated to the following special people who deserve an abundance of prayers and blessings:

Jubeka Rahman

Nabil Noor

Ayesha Khanom

Fahima Ahmed

Mahir Miah

Khadija Hassan-Ali

Hana Hassan-Ali

Mikaeel Hassan-Ali

Raheem Hassan-Ali

Eliza Miah

Anisur Rehman Usmani

Dr Zaki Rezwana Anwar

Propa Rezwana Anwar

Khurshed Begum ('Mother of Stoke')

Master Muhammad Akram

Md Roup Ali

Tamanna Ali

Nabihah Hassan

Sarfraz Ahmed Khan

Huma Sarfraz

Shaheen Shah

Aabidah Rahman

Simrah Ahmed

Faizul Hussain

Zubeda Khatun

Amelia Jesmin Campbell

Amara Alice Campbell

Siyana Ayath Khandakar

Badsha Miah

Rani Begum

Kishwer Mirza

Tawfiq Hamid

Carol Welch

Qadeer Mirza

May the Almighty accept from them and bless them all.

Author's Preface

I begin by praising Allāh, the Most Merciful, Most High. I ask Allāh ﷻ to send His peace and salutations upon His final messenger, Muḥammad ﷺ, who was sent as a mercy for all creation, and upon his family and companions.

I have always had an attachment to Sūrah Yūsuf from a young age for reasons I was initially unable to articulate or explain. From simply reciting or listening to the chapter to reading the fascinating story behind it, it has always been an inspiration for me.

Having been honoured with the opportunity to teach Sūrah Yūsuf over the years and explore it in a lot of depth through classical commentaries and contemporary works, I've discovered countless gems and lessons that have grown my love for it even more. With few English commentaries available, I decided to compile this book in an attempt to make this Quranic chapter and its profound lessons accessible to a wider audience.

This book, A Beautiful Patience, is named after one of the most profound statements in Sūrah Yūsuf, "ṣabrun jamīl" (found in verses 18 and 83), and will uncover 40 contemporary life lessons from within the chapter.

This is a humble attempt at making this unique Quranic chapter accessible for the masses and relevant for the time we live in. Though there are hundreds of lessons and rulings that can be extrapolated, I have limited it to 40 for the sake of brevity and ease. I have also chosen 40 as there is a rich tradition of this in our scholarly works, particularly in the field of Ḥadīth, whereby countless scholars have compiled thematic collections of 40 Ḥadīth, known as an Arbaʿīn. With this intention, I have applied it in this instance to a book dedicated to a beautiful chapter from the Holy Qurʾān.

I pray that Allāh ﷻ accepts this effort and allows us all to become people of the Qurʾān. I ask Allāh ﷻ to make us among those who have a deep understanding of His Book and to enable us, most importantly, to act upon it.

Shabbir Hassan, Author
Rabīʾ Al-Awwal 1442 H, October 2020

Foreword

by Shaykh Hasib Noor

In the Name of Allāh, the Most Merciful, the Giver of Mercy. Allāh's peace and blessings be on the Beloved, our Prophet Muḥammad ﷺ, his family and his companions.

Sūrah Yūsuf is no doubt among one of the most riveting stories that highlights why the guidance of the Qur'ān is timeless and miraculous. The application of faith through the telling of stories is what makes Islām that much more pragmatic. The human experience is one of unique circumstances with commonalities. The story of Yūsuf ﷺ, with its captivating lessons, makes it even more relatable as it is a true story of an ideal one can hope to aspire to.

Shaykh Shabbir Hassan has done a phenomenal job deriving timeless lessons that can speak to the human experience in our own modernity and individual circumstances.

The Qur'ān's miracle is in showing that only the Omnipotent Almighty is capable of sharing stories that may have occurred in a specific time but whose guidance is timeless to all who read it. The levels of discourse, viewpoints and very real problems it addresses makes it as applicable as when it was revealed 1,400 years ago.

Humanity is consistently in need of refining the soul and rectifying the content of character.

It is in my hopes that you, the reader, will benefit from this book something far greater than simply what has been gathered in text. It is my hope that this book teaches you how to reflect over guidance, accepting it in an act of spiritual purification and finding the light of faith which, in this world, we all desperately need.

It is precisely this light that shines bright from the story of Yūsuf ﷺ. It shows us the darkness of estrangement, toxic relationships, confinement, grappling with desire, overcoming lust, struggling through adversity when standing for the truth, unwavering trust in the Almighty, blessings born out of affliction, seeing the wisdom of the Divine in the most trying of circumstances, freeing oneself from the shackles of malice by accepting redemption to those who committed wrong and societal rectification, all founded in the faith that the Almighty is the source of guidance & enlightenment and has made believers successors thereof.

It is by no accident that the completion of this book, A Beautiful Patience, took place in Ramadan, the month of the Qur'ān. The Almighty's wisdom is found in the astute awareness of the subtleties of life. Ramadan is the month of reciting and reflecting over the Qur'ān in hopes of achieving consciousness of the Almighty in one's journey of spiritual refinement. One seeks to find depth in the conversation of the Almighty to creation, the Qur'ān, and one's own response to the Almighty, supplication and prayer. One seeks forgiveness and mercy through the heavenly sent words of the Divine, the Qur'ān. It is in this regard that the great Hanbali scholar Ibn al-Jawzī made an astute correlation between Ramadan and Yūsuf ﷺ. He said: "The month of Ramadan to the other months is like Yūsuf ﷺ to his brothers. Just like Yūsuf ﷺ was the most beloved son to Ya'qūb ﷺ, Ramadan is likewise the most beloved month to Allāh ﷻ. Just as Allāh ﷻ forgave eleven brothers through the supplication of one (Yūsuf ﷺ), He forgives eleven months with the du'ā of one (Ramadan)." (Bustān Al Wā'iẓin)

May we find light through this blessed book and may it be a means of reflection that rectifies and elevates our spiritual state, refines our character and grants us mercy, forgiveness, proximity and nearness to our Maker.

Hasib Noor, Founder & Teacher—The Legacy Institute
Ramadan 1442 H, May 2021

On the darkest of days, and during the toughest of trials, take heart in knowing that Allāh will find a way out for those who are mindful of Him.

⟶⟶ Introduction ⟵⟵

S ūrah Yūsuf is the 12th chapter (sūrah) in the Qurʾān and
has been named after the great Prophet of God, Yūsuf 🕮
(Joseph). Yūsuf 🕮 came from one of the most noble of
lineages; his father was Prophet Yaʿqūb 🕮 (Jacob), son of
Prophet Isḥāq 🕮 (Isaac), son of Prophet Ibrāhīm 🕮 (Abra-
ham). References are made to these distinguished prophets
numerous times throughout this unique chapter. The story
of Yūsuf 🕮 is one of heartbreak and sorrow and is centred
around the themes of patience and success in the face of
trials, providing much hope and inspiration for its readers.

What makes this chapter so unique is the manner in
which it was revealed and how the story is told. Many
scholars of the Qurʾān uphold that this sūrah was revealed
in its entirety, all at once, detailing the story of Yūsuf 🕮 in a
chronological order from his childhood to his demise. There
is no other chapter in the Qurʾān that places such an in-depth
focus on the story of one single prophet in the way that this
chapter does. Rather, stories of prophets, such as Mūsā 🕮
(Moses), Sulaymān 🕮 (Solomon) and Yūnus 🕮 (Jonah), are
mentioned sporadically throughout the Qurʾān.

This story is given the honorary title "the best of stories"
or "*aḥsan al-qaṣaṣ*" (12:3) for a number of reasons. Though

this should take nothing away from the other stories in the Qur'ān which are all unique in their own way, this particular chapter has an unmatched style with a plethora of lessons one can derive. Taking us through the life of a young boy who is destined for a great future, it is perhaps one of the most relatable stories across all times, especially in this day and age.

Sūrah Yūsuf is a Meccan (Makkī) chapter, meaning it was revealed prior to the migration (*hijrah*) to Madinah. Many scholars observe how the majority of the Meccan chapters consist of stories of previous prophets and nations and emphasise the core aspects of faith. This would mainly include the importance of devotion to one God (*tawḥīd*) and the condemnation of ascribing partners to Him (*shirk*). It would establish the message (*risālah*) brought by the prophets of God, upon them be peace, and would serve as a means of good news for the believers and a warning for the disbelievers. It would also confirm the eternal life to come (*ākhirah*) and highlight important morals and values that each individual should work towards. For the first thirteen years in Makkah since the beginning of revelation, these were the key messages that were sent down. It was only after the migration to Madinah that God would reveal legislations and rulings pertaining to prayer, fasting and dress code, amongst other things. This was when the lawful and unlawful were clarified, and there was exceptional wisdom behind this since the believers were now established in their faith and ready for the next phase. By understanding this nuance, we can appreciate the context of this Quranic chapter to a far better degree.

The nature of storytelling in the Qur'ān is such that it does not always provide every bit of detail, including the names of individuals and places, and sometimes it may even skip through a number of years from one verse to the next. This is no different with Sūrah Yūsuf, though it may be more detailed than any other chapter. Because the Qur'ān provides us with what is important, it never dwells on the unnecessary bits of information that we may be curious to know about. Rather, it provides us with exactly what we need to know so that we may learn and reflect. For instance, one can look up what the names of Yūsuf ﷺ's eleven brothers were or who he eventually got married to, but the fact of the matter is that these details are not entirely relevant to the core message of the *sūrah*. The Qur'ān has given us this amazing story to contemplate over, a chapter which consists of 111 verses containing everything we need to better ourselves.

With the intention of learning and reflecting, we'll now proceed with our journey through the magnificent story of Prophet Yūsuf ﷺ, as told through Sūrah Yūsuf. With the name of Allāh, exalted is He, we begin.

Though Sūrah Yūsuf
covers a variety of themes,
at its crux lies the beauty
of patience in the face
of hardship.

1

Finding Solace in Revelation

Sūrah Yūsuf is a chapter that was undoubtedly a means of consolation for Prophet Muḥammad ﷺ, especially during one of the hardest periods of his life. In the 10th year post-revelation, the Prophet ﷺ was undergoing some of the greatest trials he had experienced since being granted prophethood. This year was so strenuous upon him that it came to be known as ʿĀm al-Ḥuzn, or the Year of Sorrow.

During this time, Prophet Muḥammad ﷺ endured two of his biggest losses—the passing of his beloved wife and backbone, Khadījah ﷺ, and the death of his uncle and father-figure, Abū Ṭālib. Roughly a month apart in their demise, the Prophet ﷺ was heartbroken by both losses, as he had now lost his internal and external support. As such, chapters like Sūrah Yūsuf were pivotal for him to reflect on in these circumstances.

Our Prophet ﷺ was no stranger to the adverse conditions of life. In fact, he was raised as an orphan due to his father ʿAbdullāh passing months before his birth. He lost his mother, Āminah, at the tender age of six after he had just begun to create fond memories with her. Not many years had passed until he lost his esteemed grandfather, ʿAbd al-Muṭṭalib, for whom it is reported he wept much and had vivid memories of. This shaped the Messenger's outlook on life from an early age ﷺ, teaching him that there were no guarantees in this temporal world and that all had been decreed by God Himself.

Though Sūrah Yūsuf covers a variety of themes, at its crux lies the beauty of patience in the face of hardship. By exploring the life of Prophet Yūsuf ﷺ throughout this

The Prophet ﷺ was heartbroken by the losses of his wife and uncle, as he lost his internal and external support. Chapters like Sūrah Yūsuf were pivotal for him to reflect on in such difficult circumstances.

chapter, our Beloved ﷺ is given the opportunity to see that despite the hardships that weighed down so heavily on his heart, his brothers before him went through similar, if not greater, trials and if they could carry themselves through it and come out stronger, then so could he. It is for this reason that the Prophet ﷺ is told in the preceding chapter Sūrah Hūd: "And We relate to you the stories of the Messengers to reassure your heart…" (11:120).

As mentioned, our Prophet ﷺ required assistance from the Divine after having experienced one of the most difficult years of his mission and his entire life. He eventually found solace through this revelation, and we too can find comfort in the Qur'ān knowing that we have been promised relief with hardship. All it takes is for us to turn to God, and though the Prophet ﷺ received direct revelation to stabilise his heart, we can still refer to this

Prophet Muhammad ﷺ found solace through the revelation, of the Qur'ān, and we too can find comfort in it knowing that we have been promised relief with hardship.

same revelation for guidance and inspiration when we
need it the most.

If the most beloved creation of God, the prophets, were
tested, then where does that leave us? Prophet Muḥammad ﷺ
confirmed that it would be the most beloved to Allāh ﷻ who
would experience the greatest of tests, then the next degree
of those closest to them and so on.[1] It is said that some of
the righteous individuals of the past would get worried
when they were not being tested due to it being a sign of
one's proximity to the Creator! We should never see these
tests as a burden, rather, we should see it as an opportunity
to recognise our Lord better, a chance to test our resolve and
find solace in revelation.

1   Jāmiʿ al-Tirmidhī, Chapters on Zuhd

LESSON

2

Dream Big

It always begins with a dream. Prophet Yūsuf ﷺ was granted a dream at a young age, as demonstrated by the word *ru'yā* in verse 5, which is a vision or something that is seen. What was this dream? The vision was enough to leave anyone puzzled and confused, and even more so for an innocent child like Yūsuf ﷺ. He explains to his father, Prophet Yaʿqūb ﷺ: "O my dear father, I dreamed of eleven stars and the sun and the moon—I saw them all bow down before me" (12:4).

The whole story is based around the dream of Yūsuf ﷺ which ultimately shaped his future and it allowed his determination to remain unwavering in his life.

Yūsuf ﷺ knew that his dream was not a normal one, and the advice of his dear father would always echo in his mind that he had a great future ahead of him.

Bearing in mind that Ya'qūb ﷺ was a prophet and wise man, he realised the true nature of this dream. This was no ordinary vision, rather it was a gift from God and a prophecy of the magnificent future lying in wait for Yūsuf ﷺ.

The whole story, without a doubt, is based around this one dream which ultimately shaped the future of Yūsuf ﷺ and allowed his determination to remain unwavering. In fact, towards the end of the story we see how his dream is finally fulfilled. This is duly acknowledged by Yūsuf ﷺ when he says: "This is the fulfilment of the dream I saw long ago, my Lord has made it come true" (12:100).

What is powerful about this is how many decades had passed between Yūsuf ﷺ first seeing this dream as a child and the dream finally materialising when he held an honourable post in Egypt. He realised that if he were to achieve something remarkable, then it would require a great deal of patience, strength and fortitude to stay firm on his chosen path. He suffered many defeats along the way, underwent difficult trials and could have easily swayed, but there was always something he could look back on to make him realise what his potential was. He knew at the back of his mind that this dream was not a normal one, and the advice of his dear father would always echo in his mind that he had a great future ahead of him.

Although scholars agree that the dreams of the prophets are indeed a revelation from God, we can always set our own visions and have our own personal dreams. This dream should entail attaining goodness in this life and the next. More importantly, however, we should work towards this vision without expecting short-term results and successes. It is in the nature of humans to be tested, and these tests and

The mindset of a believer is to aim high and deliver results in this life—but more importantly, to work and prepare oneself for the ultimate life, the Akhirah. It all starts with a dream.

small defeats will help shape us in the long-term, through the will of God, so we can best fulfil our dreams.

It is befitting for the faithful to have big dreams and lofty aspirations. One of the righteous once said: "Work for this world as if you will live forever and prepare for your hereafter as if you will die tomorrow". This is the mindset of a believer—to aim high and deliver results in this life— but more importantly, to work and prepare oneself for the ultimate life, the *ākhirah*. And never forget, it all starts with a dream.

Confiding in Loved Ones

The obscurities of dreams are often such that even when experiencing extreme feelings on either end of the spectrum we are overwhelmed by the desire to tell someone we can trust and confide in, free of judgement.

Young, impressionable and entirely confused by the gravity of the dream he had just seen, Yūsuf ☙ was no exception to this human desire to understand and be understood. His first instinct after experiencing this dream was to tell the person dearest to him—his beloved father, Yaʿqūb ☙. In verse 4, Yūsuf ☙ uses compassion and affection when addressing his father as "*yā abati*" (O my dear father), and from this we see that his heart is entirely soft for this person whom he places the most trust in. Yūsuf ☙ is then advised by his father in the following verse to "relate nothing of this dream" to his

brothers. Adopting a more objective stance, Ya'qūb 🕮
is able to envision the ways in which his sons may have
reacted to news of this dream, something Yūsuf 🕮 may
not have been able to consider clearly. This is often the case
when we actively speak to others about the issues we are
experiencing—they are able to see things from a different
perspective and advise us accordingly.

More often than not, help is out there for us amongst
our loved ones, should we wish to open ourselves up to it.
Choosing to accept the help of our loved ones by confiding in
them is half the battle, but it is one worthy of doing. While
we are encouraged to pray to Allāh 🕮 about any and all of the
things we experience, good or bad, we must also trust that
He has provided the means for us to grow in our immediate
circles by speaking to those whom we love and trust.

It is often the case when we
actively speak to others about
the issues we are experiencing,
they are able to see things
from a different perspective
and advise us accordingly.

While we are encouraged to pray to Allāh ﷻ about all of the things we experience, we must also trust that He has provided the means for us to grow in our immediate circles by speaking to those whom we love and trust.

This is in no way a new concept that is isolated from the experiences of our beloved Prophet Muḥammad ﷺ. We strive to emulate the beauty of his character in our daily lives and yet let ourselves forget that at the very beginning of his prophethood, he was placed in a position of extreme distress. When experiencing the first revelation, the appearance of the Archangel Jibrīl ﷺ (Gabriel) shook him to his very core. The sheer shock and fear that our Prophet ﷺ experienced led him to his most trusted and loved friend, his wife Khadījah ﷺ. She covered him until his fear passed and reassured him with her famous words: "By Allāh, Allāh will never disgrace you!".[2] She comforted and consoled him

---

2   Ṣaḥīḥ al-Bukhārī, Book of Revelation

with loving words until his heart was softened again and ready to move forward with his new mission.

Our dear prophets Yūsuf 🙠 and Muḥammad ﷺ have both demonstrated to us through the experiences of their own trials that there is absolutely nothing wrong with sharing your problems with your loved ones and confiding in them as it is a means of comfort for you in trying times. Cultivate your circles of loved ones *and* trust in Allāh 🙠—the two are not mutually exclusive.

4

The Reality of Jealousy

With the lows and struggles, there will always come the highs and successes. It is natural that a person will experience some good days, whilst other days might not be the best. This is in fact confirmed by Allāh ﷻ in the Qurʾān when He says: "We deal out such days among people in turn" (3:140), meaning that human beings will experience the varying conditions of life throughout the years and not every day will be the same. Yet, though a person usually feels elation at the time of success, there is a danger that lurks from others, which often manifests itself as jealousy or envy of some sort.

Prophet Yaʿqūb ﷺ quickly realised that though his child had a great future ahead, this could potentially be dampened by the envy of his brothers who were already jealous of Yūsuf ﷺ's accolades and close relationship with him. It's for this reason that he commands Yūsuf ﷺ: "My dear son, tell your brothers nothing of this dream, or they may plot to harm you—undoubtedly, Satan is man's sworn enemy" (12:5). What would drive one's own blood to plot against them and potentially cause them harm? *Ḥasad* (jealousy)—a disease of the heart and a catalyst for destruction. Our Prophet ﷺ warned: "Beware of jealousy, for it eats away at good deeds just as fire consumes wood" (Ibn Mājah).

Jealousy is often defined as one's desire for God to remove someone else's blessing, either out of pure spite or because of their greed to have that same blessing themselves. It is a negative trait within human beings that exposes the state of one's heart. The brothers of Yūsuf ﷺ were willing to go to extremes purely based on their desire to see him fail and lose out. This teaches us that we do not always have to broadcast

Jealousy is a negative trait within human beings that exposes the state of one's heart. Our Prophet ﷺ warned: "Beware of jealousy, for it eats away at good deeds just as fire consumes wood."

our successes or blessings because there is a risk of falling prey to those who envy. At the same time, we can share it with those we trust and those that have good intentions for us. We should also be in the constant habit of seeking protection in Allāh ﷻ from such people: "[And I seek refuge] from the harm of the envier when they envy" (113:5).

As believers, we should be happy to see a fellow brother or sister prosper and succeed, whether we have any relationship with them or not. Know that God has already decreed what is good for us, therefore we are not missing out on a portion of our destiny if someone else is enjoying theirs. We should in fact pray for them whilst simultaneously praying that God continues to give us the best outcomes in life, as well as seeking refuge in Him from those with evil intentions. If at any point

Next time we have ill feelings when hearing about someone else's success, we should really check ourselves. If this feeling of envy is not remedied in time, there is a danger of the disease spreading across our hearts.

we do experience symptoms of jealousy in our hearts, it is incumbent that we remedy this through the remembrance of God and by seeking forgiveness from Him frequently.

What is really worth envying is a person's connection with their faith and not the material gains of this world. We are taught that envy is justified in two cases: when a person has been given knowledge of the Qur'ān so they recite it throughout the day and night, and when one has been blessed with wealth and with it they spend for Allāh ﷻ's sake throughout the day and night.[3] This type of envy comes from a good place because you do not mean bad for the other individual. Rather, you are commending them for their actions, and you are proactively trying to reach that same level, knowing that if they can achieve it, you potentially can too.

Next time we have ill feelings when hearing about someone else's success, we should really check ourselves. If this feeling of envy is not remedied in time, there is a danger of the disease spreading across our hearts. Satan is always lurking in such situations, ready to pounce when we are most vulnerable. Like the brothers of Yūsuf ﷺ, there is a high probability that we too can be made to turn against those we are closest to because of this. This is all part of Satan's many plots and strategies employed to lead us astray, therefore we cannot, under any circumstances, allow this to happen.

---

3   Ṣaḥīḥ Muslim, Book of Prayer

LESSON

5

The Ploys of Satan

I n times of joy and in the lowest of lows, we remind ourselves to continuously seek refuge from evil and those
with ill intentions. Allāh ﷻ not only reminds us of this
throughout Sūrah al-Falaq, but also when Prophet Yaʿqūb ﷺ
reiterates to Yūsuf ﷺ that it is not his brothers that he is
ultimately concerned with, but rather the ploys of the
Shayṭān (Satan): "My dear son, tell your brothers nothing
of this dream, or they may plot to harm you—undoubtedly,
Satan is man's sworn enemy" (12:5). As a prophet himself,
Yaʿqūb ﷺ was well aware of the ways in which the Shayṭān
works against humanity's innate desire to do good.

The wise man that he is, Yaʿqūb ﷺ has knowledge
bestowed upon him by Allāh ﷻ about the true nature of the
Shayṭān and the ways in which he works to destroy the very
foundations upon which our lives begin—the family unit.
As such, and with no inhibitions, Yaʿqūb ﷺ immediately
warns his son, Yūsuf ﷺ, about the Shayṭān. The Shayṭān

does not start big, but rather, quite the contrary. Like all those with some form of intelligence, he starts small and works his way up. The Shayṭān does not simply break families up, he sows discord between spouses and envy amongst siblings; he does what he can in small increments to affect individuals and their levels of faith. When the Shayṭān is usually discussed, he is often assumed to be one single individual who causes destruction up until this day, but this is a misunderstanding—an army of devilish creatures (*shayāṭīn*) exist to affect each and every single one of us, and it is not farfetched to say that they know us as well as a close companion would.

Yaʿqūb ﷺ tried to instil this awareness in Yūsuf ﷺ without placing the blame upon the brothers and by

The Shayṭān does not simply break families up, he sows discord between spouses and envy amongst siblings; he does what he can in small increments to affect individuals and their levels of faith.

acknowledging the fact that the Shayṭān will not make himself a known enemy in the most obvious of ways, he will instead break the bond that exists between the brothers by enticing them to plot against Yūsuf ﷺ.

On our race towards God, we often find that it becomes a journey into our own self wherein we are finding our faith, our purpose and, most importantly, ourselves. Both goodness and hardship come hand in hand when moving through life, and more often than not, we will find that trials are plentiful, especially as we gain proximity to our Lord. As we go and grow through these, it is important to understand that just as the brothers of Yūsuf ﷺ fell into the hands of the Shayṭān and became prone to evil, we too are susceptible to his ploys. Allāh ﷻ reminds us: "Surely Satan is an enemy to you, so take him as an enemy" (35:6). We are

It is important to understand that just as the brothers of Yūsuf ﷺ fell into the hands of the Shayṭān and became prone to evil, we too are susceptible to his ploys.

in fact reminded constantly, both in the Qur'ān and in our daily lives, that we are to know our own enemies as well as we know our own selves.

The Shayṭān infiltrates the bigger picture and ensures that he impacts the one thing that can keep us going in the darkest of hours: our relationship with Allāh ﷻ. Having made a promise to Allāh ﷻ to misguide His servants in any way, shape or form, the Shayṭān plays to our weaknesses and adds to any discord, doubts or issues we may be experiencing, often making us lose hope and abandoning Allāh ﷻ altogether. It is for this reason that we should continuously seek refuge in Allāh ﷻ from the Shayṭān and everything that makes us stray from His path.

With Knowledge, Comes Wisdom

I n verse 6, Yūsuf ﷺ is informed that He will be "chosen by God" to deliver His message, he will be gifted the ability to interpret dreams and he will join his forefathers Ibrāhīm ﷺ, Isḥāq ﷺ and his own father, Yaʿqūb ﷺ, in a chain of messengers who have been favoured and honoured by the Almighty. After Yaʿqūb ﷺ reveals the true nature of Yūsuf ﷺ's dream to him, it ends with the resounding statement: "Surely your Lord is All-Knowing, All-Wise".

Yaʿqūb ﷺ outlines two attributes of God which ultimately shape our understanding of His divine decree: that He knows exactly what He is doing through His infinite knowledge (ʿilm) and He does so with the wisdom of why and how it is best for us (ḥikmah). It was as if Yaʿqūb ﷺ was preparing Yūsuf ﷺ for what was to come because he knew that if God were to favour someone to such an extent,

He would only do so once that individual had proven themselves worthy. This would only be possible through a series of trials and tests, as was the case with his forefathers Ibrāhīm ﷺ and Isḥāq ﷺ.

An important lesson to take from this verse is though we might not know what is happening to us and what the outcome might be in life, God certainly does know for He is Al-ʿAlīm—possessing knowledge of what was and what is. Not only this, He also knows precisely why He has decreed something for us in that moment and why it is actually good because He is Al-Ḥakīm. The All-Wise. Furthermore, a deeper lesson for us to learn is that when

When we intend to impart any knowledge we may have we must do so with wisdom, for they both go hand in hand. There are many a people who possess knowledge but not wisdom, and this leads to their own downfall.

A small word said to someone with wisdom could bring that person closer to God, but another utterance, if said without wisdom, could push that person far away from Him. We should try our level best to act with wisdom.

we intend to impart any *'ilm* (knowledge) we may have we must do so with *ḥikmah* (wisdom), for they both go hand in hand. There are many a people who possess knowledge but not wisdom, and this leads to their own downfall. Allāh ﷻ says about wisdom: "He grants wisdom to whoever He wills. Whoever is given wisdom has truly been given much good" (2:269). A small word said to someone with wisdom could bring that person closer to God, but another utterance, if said without wisdom, could push that person far away from Him. It is therefore imperative that we always seek to develop a better understanding throughout our lives, and that we try our level best to act with wisdom.

Wisdom is God-given, and it is a quality that must be developed and nurtured. Age and experience play a huge role in the development of wisdom, as do good company and mentorship. As it isn't an innate virtue, anyone who is interested in trying new things and reflecting on the overall process has the ability to gain wisdom. May Allāh ﷻ make us people of true *ḥikmah*!

Outward Appearance
vs
Inward Righteousness

The very first introduction we receive of the brothers of
Yūsuf ﷺ, ten in number and senior to him, is of a boastful
nature where they claim to be an *'uṣbah*—a group of strong
men (12:8). In and of itself, the phrase means little, but in
this context, the brothers are questioning their own father
as they believed he favoured and loved Yūsuf ﷺ much more
than them. Because of this sense of entitlement they seem
to have due to their quantity, it is clear that they have fallen
prey to one of the many ploys of the Shayṭān, as mentioned
earlier. Not only have they begun to disrupt the family unit
that binds them, but they are also convinced that they are of
greater superiority because of their outward appearance.

Due to the climate we live in, wherein there is an
increasing need for aesthetic perfection, we are inclined to

ensuring our outward appearances are the most appealing
for the satisfaction of others. It is often the case that the
desire for perfection is not one that is intentional. Our
minds are made up of the thoughts and images we are
exposed to over time and so it is inevitable that we create
our perceptions of reality based on these things—we
are, after all, the physical manifestation of our innermost
thoughts. Though it is a very human thing to be enticed
by that which appears greater in value and worth, we often
forget that in the sight of Allāh ﷻ, no one human is better
than another except by way of their righteous deeds.

In Sūrah al-Ḥujurāt, we are told: "The most noble of
you in the sight of Allāh ﷻ is the most righteous among
you" (49:13). What is noteworthy here is that the word

Though it is a very human thing
to be enticed by that which
appears greater in value and
worth, we often forget that in the
sight of Allāh ﷻ, no one human
is better than another except by
way of their righteous deeds.

Allāh does not look to your bodies nor to your faces but He looks to your hearts. It is not in our numbers or our beauty that we will stand before Allāh ﷻ, but rather in strength of deeds, which will bring us up in His ranks.

"*taqwā*" has been used as a descriptor of the good character desired of us by Allāh ﷻ. *Taqwā* is not an isolated concept mentioned only in the Qur'ān, as our Prophet Muḥammad ﷺ also emphasised the importance of this heightened mindfulness of God on several occasions, the most significant being when he said: "Piety (*taqwā*) is here", while pointing at his chest thrice.[4] It is a befitting reminder that it is the purity of our hearts that increases His love for us as "Allāh does not look to your bodies nor to your faces but He looks to your hearts" (Muslim). It is not in our numbers or our beauty that we will stand before Allāh ﷻ, but rather in strength of deeds, which will bring us up in His ranks.

---

4   Ṣaḥīḥ Muslim, The Book of Virtue, Enjoining Ties of Kinship and Good Manners

Throughout the course of this Quranic chapter, both
Yūsuf 🌸 and Yaʿqūb 🌸 demonstrate an incredible amount
of sincerity in their trust in Allāh 🌸, and it is as a result
of the depth of their *taqwā* that they are so loved by Him.
Neither the beauty of Yūsuf 🌸 nor the strength in numbers
of the brothers were sufficient alone in the sight of Allāh 🌸,
but rather it is in the state of their hearts that He measured
their worth. It is for this very reason that we need to renew
our intentions daily and work on our inner selves before we
do our external appearances. Like Yūsuf 🌸 and Yaʿqūb 🌸
before us, we need to turn back to Allāh 🌸 without delay.

The Delusion of Time

One of the greatest tricks of Satan is to make us believe that we have enough time on our hands in this finite world. This leads to a vicious cycle of procrastination and carelessness, which further distances us from our Lord. We become somewhat deluded, assuming that change and betterment can wait for another day, and that we can always delay our turning back to Him. Satan makes those seeking righteousness feel lazy, and he causes those who are serious to procrastinate.[5]

This same form of delusion clouded the minds of Yūsuf ﷺ's brothers, making them resort to the lowest of actions for a short-term gain. Their envy and resentment towards their younger brother led to a discussion amongst themselves as to how they could get rid of him entirely. The first two options for them were to either "kill him", or to "abandon

---

5   Ibn al-Jawzī, Talbis Iblis

him in some foreign land" where something bad was bound to happen to him. What is interesting is the wording used by the brothers after these suggestions were made: "And after that you can become righteous people" (12:9). This deeply problematic mindset of already having the firm intention to sin with the view of repenting thereafter is what causes much destruction to the fragile hearts of God's servants. The issue is not *tawbah* (repentance) because we know that God is always open to accepting sincere *tawbah*, no matter how grave the sin. The issue is the mindset, as there is no guarantee for what is to follow once the sin has been committed.

Take the example of a person who follows this same thought process and intends to repent after their act of disobedience. It could very well be that this person finds such pleasure in the sin that they return to it multiple times thereafter. It could also be that though they repent,

'We become somewhat deluded, assuming that change and betterment can wait for another day, and that we can always delay our turning back to God.

Guilt should never overcome an individual to the point where they feel undeserving of God's mercy. In fact, it is this very guilt which should drive a person to turn back to Him without delay.

the consequences of the sin continue to haunt them for a lifetime. Or worse yet, it could be that this person never gets the opportunity to repent because God has decreed that their time in this world is up. Such is the danger of thinking in this manner, which can only lead to delusion and further problems.

It is true that the brothers of Yūsuf ﷺ eventually repented after a dark turn of events. However, what was to follow was a life full of regret, heartache and sorrow. They could never undo the wrongs committed against their father and younger brother, except through remorse and seeking forgiveness. The overarching lesson is that we should never delay in our repentance by fooling ourselves into thinking there is time. Know that God is always near, yet we are the ones who stray from Him. Likewise, know that guilt should never overcome an individual to the point where they feel undeserving of

God's mercy. In fact, it is this very guilt which should drive a person to turn back to Him without delay, for "it is He who accepts repentance from His servants and pardons bad deeds—He knows everything you do." (42:25).

The conditions of *tawbah* are three: to leave the sin, to have regret over it and to vow to never return to it again.[6] This mainly relates to sins in which a person has exceeded the limits placed by God. However, if it involves the rights of a fellow human being, then the conditions are four: the three already mentioned plus the requirement to seek forgiveness from the one you have harmed. If you have taken something away from them or damaged their property, then part of seeking their forgiveness is to return their belongings or to put things right as best as you can, even if it means compensating them. To live harmoniously, we must uphold the rights of others just as we expect them to do the same for us. Regardless of whether the sin is between you and Allāh ﷻ, such as a few missed prayers or an insincere action, or between you and a fellow human being, such as backbiting or harming them in any way, there should be no delay in turning to God sincerely, desiring His forgiveness and seeking His mercy. The doors of repentance are always open, but it is up to us to take that next step and not fall for the delusion of endless time.

---

6   Tafsīr al-Baghawī

The Importance of Consultation

The brothers of Yūsuf ﷺ, despite making a huge blunder, highlight an important aspect of decision-making in Islām as they come together as a group to discuss the ways in which they could rid themselves of the inconvenience in their life that is their younger brother. Across verses 8 to 10, the brothers use each other as a soundboard for their suggestions and though their discussion is not one that could be considered righteous or fruitful, it is important to take note that they reached a decision amongst themselves which was a far cry from some of the impulsive ones they had thought of independently ranging from "kill Yūsuf" to "banish him to another land" (12:9).

By consulting each other before acting recklessly, the brothers seem to do their own form of damage control. In hearing the gravity of each other's ideas, the voice of reason

Quite often, human impulse is dictated by the emotions that run deep within, and though we are told to trust our instincts where feelings are concerned, Allāh﷾ encourages the act of reaching out and consulting those in a position to advise.

courses through and they come to the realisation that death is perhaps a step too far and they choose an option that is not as brutal, nor one that puts blood on their own hands— at least not Yūsuf ﷺ's blood anyway. They decided instead to throw him in a well and stain his shirt with the "false blood" (12:18) of a slaughtered animal to present to their father with the hope that he would accept their narrative.

This type of discussion, one in which counsel is sought from each other, is a practice that all Muslims are encouraged to do in their daily life and is called *istishārah*. Quite often, human impulse is dictated by the emotions that run deep within, and though we are told to trust our instincts where feelings are concerned, Allāh ﷻ encourages the act of reaching out and consulting those in a position to advise. This includes, but is not restricted to, people of knowledge, those with wisdom and those who are generally trustworthy individuals. Unlike the brothers of Yūsuf ﷺ, who consulted one another knowing they had similar viewpoints and agendas, we should consult those who can offer us a fresh perspective.

The purpose of *istishārah* is to be able to grant one's own self a sense of ease, and by seeking the counsel of those who are trustworthy, it becomes less burdensome to make decisions alone. This can be seen consistently over the

While seeking counsel will provide an alternative angle to situations where judgement may have otherwise been clouded, trust in Allāh ﷻ must not be forgotten. Both need to go hand in hand in order to gain the best possible outcome.

course of our beloved Prophet Muḥammad ﷺ's life, where even in times of great turmoil and distress, he is urged by Allāh ﷻ to "consult with them [companions] about matters"[7] as it sets the heart firm upon the decision made with a complete trust that it has been divinely guided by Allāh ﷻ and therefore the best direction to take.

Albeit a discussion with the absence of any goodness and sense of righteousness, it allowed the brothers to reach a decision as decreed by Allāh ﷻ and His divine guidance. Yūsuf ﷺ was always supposed to end up in Egypt, and though his brothers caused a significant amount of emotional and psychological harm to him at such an early age, they were simply a means to an end. It was all under the discretion of Allāh ﷻ that the brothers could even come to this decision. A timely reminder that while seeking counsel will provide an alternative angle to situations where judgement may have otherwise been clouded, trust in Allāh ﷻ must not be forgotten. Both need to go hand in hand in order to gain the best possible outcome, for the one who does istikhārah (seeking God's counsel) will never fail and the one who does *istishārah* will never regret.

---

7   Qur'ān, 3:159

Offering Advice and Receiving Criticism

When it comes to giving advice, the concept of *naṣīḥah* is one that is deeply rooted in our tradition. However, *naṣīḥah* is often misunderstood entirely, or it is incorrectly applied in many instances. It is usually translated as a 'sincere advice', and though this is a fairly accurate translation, it still does not do justice to the deeper meaning this word carries. The brothers of Yūsuf ﷺ, in a desperate attempt to convince their father to permit them to take Yūsuf ﷺ out so they could pull off their scheme of throwing him into a well, say with a false conviction: "We truly wish him well" (12:11). The word for 'well-wishers' that is used in Arabic (*nāṣiḥūn*) shares the same root as the word *naṣīḥah*, which literally means 'to wish good' for someone. In fact, the Arabs would use this same word to describe the process of purifying honey, signifying that giving *naṣīḥah* to someone required a pure heart and sincere intent to bring about good for them.

The brothers of Yūsuf ﷺ were clearly not his well-wishers, nor did they intend to bring about any good for him. Drawing on this, we find nowadays that many individuals impart advice to others or do things under the guise of *naṣīḥah*, though there is seemingly nothing sincere or good about why or how they have relayed this. In fact, advice is quite often offered to put the recipient to shame or to make the one imparting it feel better about themselves. This completely goes against the true meaning of this word. Therefore, any advice given should be in a manner which brings about value for the intended recipient. Before offering advice, we should always evaluate whether this advice will be of any benefit.

As well as giving and receiving advice, criticism is also something we should brace ourselves to hear in life. Even the best of people, the messengers, were criticised whilst

Any advice given should be in a manner which brings about value for the intended recipient. Before offering advice, we should always evaluate whether this advice will be of any benefit.

When constructive criticism is given to us the right way, we should see it as an opportunity to work on our deficiencies and improve all round.

on their mission. Therefore, it is incumbent to understand how to respond to criticism, irrespective of the form it takes. Many modern psychologists mention how there are ultimately three types of criticism: destructive, irrelevant and constructive. The first two types are usually in the form of personal attacks, careless statements or words that we should not be paying any attention to. The third, however, is the only type of criticism we should welcome and most definitely take on board. In fact, constructive criticism shares the same basis as *naṣīḥah* as it is sincere and points out an improvement one can factor into their lives.

Some of the righteous scholars of the past would welcome constructive criticism to such a degree that they would go as far as to say: "May Allāh bless the one who has gifted me with the ability to see my faults", because it was a key area of development for them! Likewise, when constructive criticism is given to us the right way, we should see it as an opportunity to work on our deficiencies and improve all round. The way we react to criticism will say a lot about our true character because if we respond in a negative manner it may well mean that we need to work on ourselves and could further expose the bad traits that we carry. On the other hand, we may receive it positively and work on different areas of our own selves, be it mentally, physically or spiritually.

With Darkness Comes Light

One of the biggest factors in this story of Yūsuf ☆ is the fact that he was thrown into the "hidden depths of a well" (12:15) by his own brothers. From a place of youthful trust in the bond that he expected unconditional love from, Yūsuf ☆ was caught in a difficult position wherein there appeared to be no way out or respite. In a situation like this, it is easy to lose heart and question Allāh ☆ in an accusatory manner, but Yūsuf ☆ waited patiently and, needless to say, he was rewarded for this. In the very same verse where the darkness of the well is described, Allāh ☆ sends relief to Yūsuf ☆ in the form of divine inspiration, reassuring him that he "will remind them of this deed of theirs while they are unaware [of who you are]" (12:15). Although at the time, this revelation did not ease Yūsuf ☆'s physical predicament for he still saw no immediate escape from the well, it was still a form of spiritual relief which eased the burden on his heart as he came to know that Allāh 🕮 was not unaware of what he was enduring and that, in time, He would show him some kind of light.

The patience and endurance demonstrated by Yūsuf 🕮, despite his circumstances, is clear evidence of the oft-repeated verse: "Indeed, with hardship [will be] ease" (94:5-6). We often find ourselves wondering why we are told that ease will come with hardship rather than *after* it. The reason is simply that Allāh 🕮 has reassured us constantly throughout the Qur'ān that with each difficulty and hardship that is faced by us, there is an element of ease and good that will inevitably follow. It is by His will that we endure, it is by His will that we overcome and it is by His will that we will grow.

In Sūrah al-Baqarah, we are reminded that: "God does not burden any soul with more than it can bear" (2:286).

The patience and endurance demonstrated by 'Yūsuf 🕮, despite his circumstances, is clear evidence of the oft-repeated verse: "Indeed, with hardship (will be) ease."

It is therefore prudent for us to take comfort in this knowledge. Allāh ﷻ knows our strengths and weaknesses and only puts us in situations He knows we can bring ourselves out of through the means He has, or will, provide us with. Even on the darkest of days when we seem to be in the deepest depths of our own wells, Allāh ﷻ will provide that which we could not even fathom. He will bring forth help from where we could not even have imagined it existing.

Just like Yūsuf ﷺ, all of us at some point or another in our lives have been, or are, stuck in our own well. We have all felt some form of darkness in our lives—be it anxiety,

Even on the darkest of days when we seem to be in the deepest depths of our own wells, Allāh ﷻ will provide that which we could not even fathom. He will bring forth help from where we could not even have imagined it existing.

depression, financial issues or rocky relationships. The Shayṭān will try and convince you that there is no way you can get out because it is amongst his greatest ploys to sell you the delusion that who you used to be, or the things that brought you into this well, somehow have a greater value than the ability Allāh ﷻ possesses to bring you back out. Do not let yourself fall for this delusion. If you truly want to get out of this well, then understand that this darkness is a part of the process and the light that follows will far surpass any you will have ever seen.

Have faith in Allāh ﷻ, exercise beautiful patience and express gratitude for the ability to go and grow through these hardships, for the tree that is rooted in gratitude will only bear fruits of positivity.

LESSON

12

The Virtue of Patience

There is no doubt that this entire chapter of the Qur'ān is centred around exercising immense patience in the face of trials and displaying a high level of forbearance. As the old saying goes, 'patience is a virtue', and we believe that patience itself holds the keys to unlocking great virtues and rewards. God Himself says: "And Allāh is with the patient" (2:249), and in another verse He declares: "And Allāh loves the patient" (3:146).

The brothers of Yūsuf ﷺ conjured up a lie after leaving him in the well and told their father: "We went racing and left Yūsuf with our belongings, and a wolf devoured him!" (12:17). Upon hearing the news that his most beloved son Yūsuf ﷺ had now gone missing under the false pretence of being eaten by a wolf, Yaʿqūb ﷺ was left completely heartbroken and shaken. None can feel the pain of losing a child more than a parent, yet despite this overwhelming news he stood firm and remained composed by uttering the words: "A beautiful patience" (*sabrun jamīl*). Knowing that the rest of his sons had betrayed his trust and caused harm to their own brother, Yaʿqūb ﷺ did not once complain nor did he act hastily. Instead, he demonstrated a truly beautiful patience, which is a patience without complaining about the situation[8] and without responding in a negative manner. He ended this statement by exclaiming: "From God alone I seek help to bear what you are saying" (12:18). This highlights his utmost reliance and trust in God, and although he was distressed, he knew that it was God alone who could help him—after all, his own family had gone against him, and he was left completely alone in a vulnerable position. Yaʿqūb ﷺ's faith never deteriorated and it was exactly this that got him through this truly testing time.

'Yaʿqūb ﷺ demonstrated a truly beautiful patience, which is a patience without complaining about the situation or responding in a negative manner. He said: "From God alone I seek help to bear what you are saying."

---

8   Tafsīr al-Ṭabarī

Every human being has a different threshold of tolerance and varying levels of patience. It is, however, a key value we must work on, and to do this requires an understanding of the nature and meaning of *ṣabr* (patience). The Prophet Muḥammad ﷺ said: "Patience is at the first stroke of calamity"[9], indicating that true patience is reflected at the very moment one is struck with misfortune. At this point, one can either completely break down and react without any thought, almost like a reflex, or one can respond just as Ya'qūb ﷺ did. In fact, the linguistic definition of *ṣabr* in Arabic is to 'withhold', which is not to say one has to suffer in silence, but rather that this person withholds any negative feelings towards God and refrains from complaining. Though it is a very challenging and difficult process, a believer will always see the positives in moments of difficulty. Our Prophet ﷺ once said: "How amazing is the situation of a believer.

The good that a believer is anticipating may not be clear at one particular moment in time, but God will always do what is best for His servants.

---

9   Ṣaḥīḥ al-Bukhārī, Book of Funerals

There is good for them in everything and this applies only to a believer. If they experience any good and they are thankful, then it is good for them. And if they experience a misfortune and they are patient, it is also good for them".[10] To put it in the simplest of terms, for believers, it is a win-win situation.

The good that a believer is anticipating may not be clear at that particular moment in time, but God will always do what is best for His servants. Sometimes the most valuable lessons are learnt through the toughest of trials, and sometimes the most rewarding outcomes are gained through the harshest of conditions. Yūsuf ﷺ and Yaʿqūb ﷺ were both soon to gain a small insight into exactly how God's plan would work out and how it would ultimately favour them over time.

---

10 Ṣaḥīḥ Muslim, The Book of Zuhd

13

God's Plan

When it comes to understanding the great wisdom of God Almighty and His decision to test us the way He does in life, we only have room to speculate. God says in the Qur'ān: "Do people think once they say, 'We believe', that they will be left alone without being put to the test?" (29:2). God also explains that one of the reasons for creating life and death is "to test which of you is best in deeds" (67:2). Once we can establish that trials are a part of and form our daily lives, we can only then try to begin understanding some of the wisdoms behind this. It goes without saying that we cannot always know the reason and see the bigger picture, as this knowledge is possessed by God and God alone.

Young Yūsuf 🕮 was certainly in a confused state whilst being trapped in the hidden depths of the well, and he could not quite understand what he did to deserve a separation like this. However, what he didn't know was that God had a plan in place for him and that his patience and struggle would not go unnoticed. Simultaneously, God had already made His move, and a caravan that had originally departed from Syria (Al-Shām) was making its way to Egypt—where Yūsuf ﷺ was destined to be in the future. This group of travellers had no intention of stopping off by the well where Yūsuf ﷺ was, however, God made this caravan lose its way and end up just outside the well, exactly where He wanted them to be.[11] The stranded travellers decided that since they were now lost, it would be best for them to take some rest and revitalise themselves. They sent one of their own to fetch them some water from the well, yet to the surprise of this individual he found something he was not expecting. He screamed: "Good news, here is a boy!" (12:19) as he came across a handsome young child who was clearly distressed. It was a bittersweet moment for Yūsuf ﷺ as he was finally rescued from the darkness of the well, yet he now stood at

Once we can establish that trials are a part of and form our daily lives, we can only then try to begin understanding some of the wisdoms behind this.

---

11 Tafsīr al-Baghawī

the mercy of these complete strangers. They immediately decided to hide him and sell him as a slave, and the most suitable place for them to do this was in Egypt, in the hustle and bustle of its popular marketplaces. Yūsuf ﷺ was faced with yet another trial, yet he was better equipped for this now that God had salvaged him from the darkness of the well.

Life is such that nothing really is a coincidence. In fact, though we can be the victims of our own decisions, Allāh ﷻ has already factored in what is best for us through His sheer mercy and love. There was no way that anyone from Yūsuf ﷺ's family would rescue him from his plight, and so these strange travellers were sent to collect him and take him to his intended destination. The final destination was not the well. Rather, this was just a means to an end and a

'Life is such that nothing really is a coincidence. In fact, though we can be the victims of our own decisions, Allāh ﷻ has already factored in what is best for us through His sheer mercy and love.

stopover to strengthen Yūsuf ﷺ further. The plan all along was for Yūsuf ﷺ to actually settle in Egypt, the land he would later have authority over, and this was just one of the pieces of the puzzle to set all in motion. Thus, we should constantly be reminded of the verse: "Say: 'Nothing will ever befall us except what Allāh has destined for us. He is our Protector', so in Allāh let the believers put their trust" (9:51). Everything we are struck with in life is part of the divine decree. The word 'muṣībah' itself, though commonly translated and viewed as a 'calamity', actually shares its root with the word iṣābah which gives the meaning of an arrow hitting its target. What is then clear is that we were the intended targets of any muṣībah which afflicted us in our lives. We were supposed to go through it and grow through it. Just like the one who is struck by an arrow and goes through a recovery process, we too must heal and become stronger through our wounds before we can continue. This was not something we could have simply avoided; this was already written for us.

Whether it comes in the form of a delay, a random stranger or an unprecedented opportunity or situation, all these events can be seen as tiny pixels which are forming a bigger picture. As verse 21 concludes: "Allāh always prevails in His purpose, though most people do not realise it".

Realising Your True Value

Knowing what truly holds value and worth in our eyes will say a great deal about ourselves. Some may value beauty over character, and others will hold wealth dearer than legacy. Often times, we overvalue the wrong things and end up undervaluing ourselves in the process.

The travellers from Syria resorted to hiding Yūsuf 🕮 "as a merchandise" (12:19) and then selling him as planned. Upon their arrival in Egypt, they made a quick dash towards the marketplace where he was to be sold. Due to their desperation and apprehension, knowing that this child was not actually their property to begin with, they opted for the swiftest transaction possible. Thinking of Yūsuf 🕮 as a small and weak child, perhaps orphaned and completely abandoned with not much worth, they were disinterested and sold him for just a few coins. This is described in verse 20 when God

Our real worth is not predicated on our background, appearance or status. Rather, our worth is defined by how valuable we are seen to God and how positively we have impacted or influenced the people around us.

says: "They sold him for a paltry price, for a few silver coins, so little did they value him". The actions of these travellers highlight many of our actions and the state of our hearts; we consistently overvalue that which is insignificant in reality. What these people did not know is that they had just undersold someone so valued in the sight of God—a person who would be chosen and honoured, and an individual who would later rule the very land that was beneath their feet.

Our real worth is not predicated on our background, appearance or status. Rather, our worth is defined by how valuable we are seen to God and how positively we have impacted or even influenced the people around us. How many monarchs and leaders walked the earth with the world's treasures at their disposal yet were humiliated and forgotten over time? How many strong and powerful men trod the same paths we walk on yet were buried in the same way as the weak and despised in society? At the same time, how many individuals were there who struggled, were looked down upon and not given any attention, yet their legacy lives on today through their works, progeny and efforts? In the day and age of the internet, it is easy to become impressed with the lifestyles of certain people, which in turn has a negative effect on our own self-esteem. We end up wrongly overvaluing our peers based on their salaries and titles and in the process forget how much

'It is easy to become impressed with the lifestyles of certain people, which in turn has a negative effect on our own self-esteem. We end up wrongly overvaluing our peers based on their salaries and titles and in the process forget how much potential and value we hold.'

potential and value we hold. A famous Arab poet once said: "You deem yourself to be just a little body, yet a great universe dwells within you".

Being undersold as a slave further added to Yūsuf ﷺ's woes and miseries as he was taken advantage of at first sight. He now had to deal with the next chapter of this grim journey, which had already seemed like a lifetime for him, and naturally he began to question where he would end up next. God did not plan to humiliate or disappoint him however, as the next move would slowly place Yūsuf ﷺ in a far better situation. He was valued so much that it was no coincidence that the one awaiting him in Egypt was one of the most powerful men of the land—the Minister of Egypt himself.

LESSON

15

Escaping Fitnah

When facing a trial in life, it will either bring the best out of us or the worst. The word *'fitnah'* in Arabic is commonly used to describe a testing situation. However, this word was originally used to describe the process of purifying gold.[12] One method of purifying gold is to heat it to such a degree that it rids it of its impurities and dross, resulting in a valuable and beautiful product that we usually adorn ourselves with. Similarly, when we are tested, the heat of the situation is a means of refinement and purification for us, with the objective being that we come out better and more valuable on the other end.

In his early years, Yūsuf ﷺ had to face much *fitnah* along the way, and there appeared to be no signs of this ceasing after his arrival in Egypt. He was purchased by the Minister of Egypt, referred to as 'Al-'Azīz', and found

---

12 Rāghib al-Aṣfahānī, Mufradāt al-Qur'ān

himself currently surrounded by royalty and luxuries. From the dark pit of the well, Yūsuf ﷺ was now rewarded for his patience with the comfort of the palace and good treatment from the Minister and his family. This certainly alleviated some of his pain. However, he was now to be tested with one of his greatest trials yet, and one that would continue to bring out the best in his character.

Yūsuf ﷺ was known to be a handsome young man, with some narrations detailing that he had been given half the world's beauty[13], and over the years this developed and peaked as he reached the age of adolescence. Naturally, this would attract some unwarranted attention his way,

By remaining in a space where God's disobedience is taking place or where one's faith is at risk of being affected, we only intensify the desire to divulge in the evil that is present.

---

13 Ṣaḥīḥ Muslim, Book of Faith

but he did not once imagine that this would come from the direction of the Minister's wife. After being placed in her trust by the Minister himself, she was now prepared to betray her husband. She became infatuated with Yūsuf ﷺ, causing her to take action after a short battle of resistance. It was thus that Yūsuf ﷺ faced another moment of *fitnah* as she locked the doors and "tried to seduce him" (12:23). This was the moment of heat that he now had to overcome. The first course of action that Yūsuf ﷺ resorted to was to seek refuge in God. After all, he knew that God was testing him, and ultimately only He could be the one who could

'We can succumb to the evil or temporary enjoyment, or we can decide to stay firm and take the necessary steps to guard ourselves. By seeking refuge in God and leaving the place of sin or negativity, we will become purified and ultimately honoured by our Lord.

protect him whilst in solitude. He exclaimed: "Allāh is my refuge!" (12:23) and made mention of the good that the Minister had done to him by offering him shelter and a warm welcome, and that there was no way he could betray him. Yūsuf ﷺ was conscious of fulfilling the right of God, as well as fulfilling the rights of his fellow human beings. The second step that Yūsuf ﷺ took was to immediately look for a way out, and the most practical solution for that was to find the exit and leave the room they were in. This also teaches us another important lesson when facing this type of *fitnah*—that we should leave the place of sin and take refuge elsewhere. By remaining in a space where God's disobedience is taking place or where one's faith is at risk of being affected, we only intensify the desire to divulge in the evil that is present.

There will be no shortage of these situations in our lives, whereby we will be tested and faced with extremely difficult conditions. These moments will not only test our faith but will also test our strength and willpower. We can succumb to the evil or temporary enjoyment, or we can decide to stay firm and take the necessary steps to guard ourselves. By seeking refuge in God and leaving the place of sin or negativity, we will become purified and ultimately honoured by our Lord, as we shall soon see was the case for Yūsuf ﷺ.

16

Taqwā Opens Up Doors

Throughout this chapter, there is a heavy emphasis on the importance of *taqwā* as an integral part of a Muslim's character, as demonstrated by both Yaʿqūb ﷺ and his beloved son, Yūsuf ﷺ. To truly understand the term *taqwā*, commonly translated as 'God consciousness', there is a need to contextualise it within the framework of its linguistic root *'wiqāyah'*. The word *wiqāyah* itself means to guard and protect oneself from all that is evil, harmful and sinful, in turn indicating that *taqwā* must also encompass this, alongside an active awareness of the omnipresence of Allāh ﷻ.

Our beloved Prophet ﷺ was no stranger to emphasising the importance of this awareness and mindfulness of Allāh ﷻ. Amongst his advice to ʿAbdullāh Ibn ʿAbbās, may Allāh ﷻ be pleased with him, was: "O Ibn ʿAbbās, be wary of Allāh wherever you might be, and you will find Him to be there"

(Al-Tirmidhī). Though this may seem simple in theory, it is often very difficult to remind oneself that Allāh ﷻ is present and aware of all that we know and know not. Behind closed doors, it is easy to delude oneself into believing that in that particular moment only those in that room are aware of your actions and thoughts. This is the very same delusion that clouded the judgement of the Minister's wife when she was overcome by Yūsuf ﷺ's beauty and attempted to seduce him. It is demonstrated, with no shadow of a doubt, that "she bolted the doors and said, 'Come to me!'" (12:23). What is important to take note of here is the emphasis on the way the

'It is often very difficult to remind oneself that Allāh ﷻ is present and aware of all that we know and know not. Behind closed doors, it is easy to delude oneself into believing that in that particular moment only those in that room are aware of your actions and thoughts.

door was closed. The doors were not just shut or a blockade put up, rather they were bolted in a way that indicates there was no way in or out unless active effort was put in to open them again. In this very moment, the human instinct of desire and temptation could very well take over man, but for Yūsuf ﷺ it was his *taqwā* that saved him from his own self for "he would have succumbed to her if he had not seen evidence (*burhān*)[14] of his Lord" (12:24).

As mentioned, if we are to avoid committing a sin, it is in our best interests to leave the place of evil. This is exactly

Yūsuf ﷺ made the active decision to avoid sin with a conscious awareness of Allāh's presence, and though it was not the easiest situation to be in, Allāh ﷻ physically helped him out of it.

---

14 Classical scholars have differed over the interpretation of what this 'evidence' was. Some say that Prophet Yūsuf was shown a vision of his father, Prophet Yaʿqūb, whilst in the room (Tafsīr Ibn Kathīr). Imam al-Ṭabarī argues that there is no conclusive evidence either way, so we leave it ambiguous as God has left it.

the choice Yūsuf ﷺ made, but it was not one that was made easy for him: "They raced for the door, and she tore his shirt from the back" (12:25). This moment of hardship came with its rightful ease, and he was rewarded for his *taqwā* as they met her husband at the door. Though in first reading, it does not necessarily seem like a reward, that is, to be found in this compromising situation by the Minister, but one must remember that the doors were bolted shut and it is nothing short of a miracle that with no need for a key or great effort to open them, Yūsuf ﷺ was discovered and found a way out.

Taking this into account allows for the realisation that by having *taqwā*, doors are opened by Allāh ﷻ in the most literal sense of the word. Yūsuf ﷺ made the active decision to avoid sin with a conscious awareness of His presence, and though it was not the easiest situation to be in, Allāh ﷻ physically helped him out of it. In the very same way, when we are faced with trials and tribulations which threaten to shake us to our core and test everything we stand for, an awareness of the omnipresence of Allāh ﷻ will allow us to have some ease of mind, knowing that He is aware of all that we do, and He will help us find a way out.

On the darkest of days, and during the toughest of trials, take heart in knowing that "Allāh will find a way out for those who are mindful of Him" (65:2).

The Degrees of Love

One of the most natural emotions every human will experience at some point in their lifetime is that of love and affection. What starts off as an attachment, develops into something deeper and has the potential to grow into something beautiful. Some linguists even mention the link between *ḥubb* (love) and *ḥabbah* (seed) in the Arabic language and their shared, close meaning—a seed can also grow and develop into something quite wonderful, bearing delicious fruits and produce. It is, however, also noteworthy that this love can go through an exponential growth, which could potentially lead to an unhealthy and unbalanced obsession in one's heart. It is for this reason that our Prophet ﷺ said: "Your love for a thing has the ability to make you blind and deaf" (Abū Dawūd). That is to say, a person can become quite blinded to the truth and lose their senses when they are overwhelmed by their desires and overcome by this sense of passionate love (ʿishq).

Such was the case with the Minister's wife, as Allāh 🕮 describes her love in a negative way—one driven by her desires and passion. When some of the influential women of Egypt discussed what had taken place between her and Yūsuf 🕮, they said: "Love for him has consumed her heart!" (21:30). The word *shaghaf,* which is used to describe her feelings for Yūsuf 🕮 in this verse, also happens to be the same word used for the pericardium—the layer of membrane that covers and encloses the heart of each human being. Her feelings were so deep for Yūsuf 🕮 that it even penetrated this covering in her heart, causing her to bypass her feelings for her own husband and attempt to entice the young man in front of her. This feeling is also known as infatuation or lust, whereby a person becomes attracted to the beauty that they see and has only a physical desire for it. This type of love is not a good one, rather it is a temporary yet overpowering feeling which can cloud one's judgement and drive them towards evil.

A person can become quite blinded to the truth and lose their senses when they are overwhelmed by their desires and overcome by a sense of passionate love ('ishq).

Though he had the opportunity
to fall into sin and give in to
the temptation, he was steadfast
and remained conscious of
God. This act displayed his
ultimate love for his Lord over
any type of temporary desire
or satisfaction.

Throughout this story, there are different degrees of love mentioned. Right at the beginning, we find the love that a father has for a son in the dialogue between Yaʻqūb ﷺ and Yūsuf ﷺ. We then find the love that siblings have for one another, which was transformed into envy by Satan. We also find the love that a person can have for a complete stranger, as we saw with the Minister when he first brought Yūsuf ﷺ home. Now we find this passionate love that the Minister's wife had for him. These are all varying levels of love which can be seen as good in some cases and bad in others. There is no doubt, however, that the strongest and most noble type of love is found in this passage, whereby Yūsuf ﷺ displays his love for his Lord, Allāh ﷻ.

Though he had the opportunity to fall into sin and give in to the temptation, he was steadfast and remained conscious of God. This act displayed his ultimate love for his Lord over any type of temporary desire or satisfaction. Putting Allāh ﷻ first and loving Him is what our aim in life should be, as opposed to attaching our hearts to worldly things. Though it is not intrinsically wrong to love someone or something, fully attaching our hearts to what is temporary and finite will only be a cause of heartbreak for us when it is gone. However, by attaching our hearts to the Eternal we will find none other than solace and peace in our lives, which we are very much in need of.

LESSON

18

Keeping Good Company

There is no denying that as we go and grow through life there is a real human need for companionship. We are inherently social beings who thrive, in all senses of the word, on good company and through our social interactions. This is often equated to our growth as a society, but the truth of this was present even in the life of Yūsuf ﷺ. When faced with his trial with the wife of the Minister, we see the devastating effects the wrong kind of companionship can have on both an individual and society as a whole.

Having become the talk of the town after being caught in a compromising situation "trying to seduce her slave boy" (12:30), the Minister's wife takes it upon herself to prove a point to the esteemed women of Egypt, in either a bid for revenge or redemption. She set out to prove that she was not "clearly mistaken" (12:30) as they had suggested, but rather, that they themselves would be "stunned by his beauty" (12:31) and fall victim to the very same desires. Inviting them all over to her residence under the pretext of a banquet, she summons for Yūsuf 🕮, and as the story goes, they were all so taken aback by his beauty that they heedlessly cut their own hands, exclaiming: "Good God! He cannot be mortal! He must be a noble angel!" (12:31). More importantly, they not only understood why she had acted the way that she did, but they also took it that one step further by excusing her actions and justifying that which is immoral.

This encouragement of unacceptable behaviour could have been avoided had the Minister's wife chosen her companions wisely. Though everything happens by the will of our Lord, it is necessary for us to weigh up the pros and cons of things before they are a part of our lives, especially

Not only should our company be righteous but also positive, meaning that we feel uplifted by being in their presence and do not feel like we are stuck in a toxic or negative environment.

if the pros of the thing in question far outweigh the cons. In this particular context, there is a need to acknowledge that good companionship comes with many benefits. These range from being as simple as a hand in need during trying times to being as important as a physical reminder of our relationship with God as we walk through life. This type of companionship is encouraged by Allāh ﷻ in the Qur'ān as He says: "You who believe, be mindful of God and be with the truthful" (9:119), making the relationship between having *taqwā* and keeping good companions as clear as day.

Our beloved Prophet ﷺ continued to emphasise the importance of keeping good company when he said: "A man follows the religion of his friend, so each one should consider whom he makes his friend" (Abū Dawūd).

Find the companions who bring you back to your truest self and keep you in check. They are the people in whose presence we will struggle to sin, for their very essence guides us towards good in all that we do in life.

Keeping this in mind, it is no doubt better for one to be alone than to be in the company of those who encourage us to transgress against our own selves. Both prophetic traditions and the Qur'ān place a great deal of importance on this type of companionship, serving as the inspiration we need to ensure our lives are filled with people whose presence remind us of God. Not only should our company be righteous but also positive, meaning that we feel uplifted by being in their presence and do not feel like we are stuck in a toxic or negative environment.

Find the companions who bring you back to your truest self and keep you in check. These are the people in whose presence we will struggle to sin, for their very essence guides us towards good in all that we do in life.

Consistency in Character

Throughout the course of our lives, we strive to fill it with the companionship and presence of those who inspire us to do good and move closer to Allāh ﷻ. However, there comes a point where we must ask ourselves if we are the type of people whose company we would actively seek out? Being a good human lies at the crux of our identities as Muslims who live in His way, and so we must strive to be this way in any and every case.

Yūsuf ﷺ was faced with situations which put him amongst people who are not entirely good or have the best of intentions, but this in no way allowed his character to waiver. Although his innocence had already been proven by the fact that his shirt had been torn from behind (12:28), Yūsuf ﷺ was still sent to prison. It was in fact something he himself desired: "My Lord! I would prefer prison to what these women are calling me to do." (12:33). A mutual agreement between him and the Minister was thus reached—he would be back again once things had cooled off slightly and that he would only be in prison "for a while" (12:35).

Despite the circumstances, he presented himself to be of the *Muḥsinīn* (a person of excellence) on almost every occasion (12:36). The most pressing example of this was during his time in the prison where he was surrounded by those who were considered to be of the lowest social ranks at the time, and yet, he referred to them at all times as "my fellow prisoners" (12:39), demonstrating the utmost respect to even the outcasts of society. Even in a situation that was displeasing for him, Yūsuf ﷺ maintained his sublime character. Days led to weeks and weeks led to months as Yūsuf ﷺ found himself in the cell for much longer than initially anticipated.

Yūsuf's ﷺ immense level of consistency in his character is what helped win over the hearts of the people around him and, most importantly, earned him a high rank in the life to come.

Kindness and good character settle in the hearts of the people more than words ever could. Aspire to be the person who leaves goodness in all the lives you touch with the essence of your character and actions.

Often, we find that it is easy to display our best selves and the best of our character in times of goodness and ease, or to be of excellence when we are in the presence of those who are of a higher social status. Though this is a good trait to have, it is better for the believer to be excellent in both morals and conduct in all walks of life and with all people, no matter who they may be. This reminder to display good character at all times is demonstrated continuously by Yūsuf 鑫—even as he later goes from the lowly social status as a prisoner to one of authority and high status in society, people continued to say the very same thing: "We can see that you are a person of excellence" (12:78). This immense level of consistency in his character is what helped win over the hearts of the people around him and, most importantly, earned him a high rank in the life to come. After all, our

Prophet ﷺ informed us that those closest to him on the Day of Resurrection will be those who were best in character,[15] which makes it even more enticeful for us to adopt a consistent level of excellent character.

Much like Prophet Yūsuf ﷺ before us, we must learn how best to show goodness at all times and become a people of excellence (iḥsān) as actions speak far louder than words, thus making this the most appropriate way to propagate the true message of our faith, even prior to dialogue. Kindness and good character settle in the hearts of the people more than words ever could. Aspire to be the person who leaves goodness in all the lives you touch with the essence of your character and actions.

---

15 Jāmiʿ al-Tirmidhī, Chapters on Righteousness and Maintaining Ties of Kinship

Wisdom in Daʿwah

After establishing that the best form of spreading the beautiful message of faith is through one's actions, it is equally as important to understand how best to engage with others in dialogue when giving *daʿwah*. The term *daʿwah* literally means to 'invite', and in a more general context, it would refer to the act of inviting others to the faith. As God Almighty says in the Qurʾān: "Call to the way of your Lord with wisdom and good counsel..." (16:125), signifying the importance of not just robotically uttering a few words and verses, but rather tailoring it to each individual and doing so in a beautiful and measured way.

When Yūsuf ﷺ was requested to interpret the dreams of the two companions in prison, one of whom had seen himself "pressing wine" and one of whom had seen himself carrying bread on his head "from which birds were eating" (12:36), he saw this as an opportunity to invite them to the correct way of life. Yūsuf ﷺ had done his duty presenting

Yūsuf ﷺ not only displayed his wisdom by waiting for the right moment to give them da'wah with his carefully selected words, but he also addressed them respectfully and with good counsel.

his faith through his actions, which is why it resulted in these two young men feeling comfortable enough to approach him and even compliment his character in the first place. They had a level of trust in him, and it was only right for him to capitalise on this. He also understood that they were now in need of him and since he had their attention, he wanted to help them understand the true purpose of life with the hope that they would leave their life of crime and disbelief. It is for this reason why he began giving them *da'wah* and presented rational arguments to make them reflect. One of the statements he makes, as recorded in verse 39, is: "O my fellow prisoners, would many diverse gods be better than God, the One, the All Powerful?". Through this, he not only displayed his wisdom by waiting for the right moment to give them *da'wah* with his carefully selected words, but he also addressed them respectfully and with good counsel. He then concluded the interpretation of their dreams, as promised, informing the first that he would be freed, going on to serve his master wine, and the other would be crucified for his crime, resulting in birds eating bread from his head. Yūsuf ﷺ then made a request to the former of the two to make mention of his name when he returns to the palace so he himself could be released from prison. By this stage, Yūsuf ﷺ had already spent "a while" (12:35) in prison, which had now prolonged into "several years" (12:42).

The lesson for us here is that *da'wah* should be given with wisdom and good words. It is not appropriate for us to address others in a harsh manner or to quickly judge them, even if our beliefs or creeds differ. In fact, when Prophet Mūsā ﷺ was sent to address the Pharaoh, an

Da'wah should be given with wisdom and good words. Wisdom must be applied when relaying the message of our faith or the consequences can be quite severe if we do not.

open tyrant and oppressor who had the audacity to refer to himself as the "supreme lord" (79:24), he was commanded by Allāh ﷻ to speak to him with "gentle words" (20:44) so that perchance he may be reminded. This, of course, does not always work. However, it is befitting for a believer to embody these characteristics when dealing with others. Wisdom must be applied when relaying the message of our faith and, as discussed in Chapter 6, the consequences can be quite severe if we do not. One form of wisdom is to ensure the person you are engaging with is comfortable with you and knows you to an extent, else there is a lack of reciprocation. After all, every messenger was sent to his own people, and they lived amongst them, speaking their language and understanding their culture. This is key when it comes to understanding and engaging with others, and this is precisely what Prophet Yūsuf ﷺ did in prison.

LESSON 21

The Importance of Gratitude

Once, 'Umar Ibn al-Khaṭṭāb ☼, the Commander of the Faithful, heard a man making an unusual supplication. The man was saying: "My Lord! Make me from the few!", which led 'Umar ☼ to address this and ask him why he was making a supplication that he had not heard the Prophet ﷺ specifically make himself. The man responded to this by quoting the verse from the Qur'ān wherein Allāh ☼ says: "Only a few of My servants are truly grateful" (34:13), explaining that he wanted to be from this minority of grateful servants. 'Umar began weeping thereafter and exclaimed: "Everyone is more knowledgeable than you O 'Umar!".[16]

A similar verse is found in Sūrah Yūsuf when Yūsuf ﷺ is addressing the companions of the prison in verse 38:

---

16 Tafsīr al-Qurṭubī

"However most people are ungrateful". The reality is that we have been blessed with so much that although it is almost impossible to be grateful for every single thing that we have, we as human beings and servants of God often don't even try. The concept of *shukr* (gratitude) is an important one, and without it we are but aimless individuals who do not appreciate the blessings bestowed upon us. God is not in need of our thanks—it is us who are in need of thanking Him. Allāh ﷻ says: "If you are thankful, I will certainly give you more" (14:7), which shows it is in fact us who benefit from being thankful. Whether it's being grateful for the food we eat, the comfort we enjoy or our family around us, it is imperative that we display this in whatever form we can. It was in fact Prophet Nūḥ ﷺ (Noah) who said to God: "How can I be grateful when just the ability to be grateful is

The concept of gratitude is an important one, and without it we are but aimless individuals who do not appreciate the blessings bestowed upon us. God is not in need of our thanks – it is us who are in need of thanking Him.

The highest form of shukr is through one's limbs, by which a servant is grateful through their actions. For one to reflect in their limbs what they feel in their hearts and utter with their tongues is a gratitude of the highest degree.

another blessing from You?", to which God replied: "Nūḥ, now you have understood the true nature of gratitude!".[17]

There are different forms of gratitude, the first of which originates from the heart. In other words, the lowest level of *shukr* is to at least acknowledge the blessing in your heart and be content with it. The next level of *shukr* is through the tongue, whereby one verbally gives thanks and praises the one who is deserving of it. An example of this in our context would be to frequently recite statements such as 'All praise and thanks belong to Allāh' (*Alḥamdulillāh*). The highest

---

17 Tafsīr Ibn Kathīr

form of *shukr* is through one's limbs, by which a servant
is grateful through their actions. For one to reflect in their
limbs what they feel in their hearts and utter with their
tongues is a gratitude of the highest degree.

From this we understand that if Allāh ﷻ has given us
wealth, then we thank Him for it by spending it in His way
and not being excessive with it. If He has blessed us with
health, we use that to serve Him to the best of our abilities.
If He has given us time, then we use it wisely as each
passing minute is a minute lost and never to be returned to
us again. And ultimately, if Allāh ﷻ has blessed us with life,
then the best way of being grateful for this is to make use of
it and draw nearer to Him with every breath that we take.
From the moment we wake up in the morning, we should
be in a state of gratitude and not waste any opportunity that
comes our way. After all, God says: "We will recompense
those who are grateful" (3:145). May He make us from His
few servants who are grateful and appreciative!

Addressing People with Kindness

The epitome of one's character is defined through their dealings with other people. The extent to which a person feels valued in your company and how you communicate with them will sum up their feelings and overall respect towards you. One way to give someone the respect they deserve is through the way we address them. Our Prophet ﷺ taught us: "Deal with people according to their status" (Abū Dāwūd), which shows that though we must equally respect every human being, the level of respect may differ from individual to individual based on their social standing or relation to you. A basic example of this is how a child would address their mother or father, and how they would address their siblings. Though both deserve their own share of respect, it is natural that one's parents will receive a different level of reverence in comparison to their siblings or friends. It is equally as important not to address anyone in a manner

'It is important that as people of faith we make each other feel valued, and this can only be done through good manners and etiquettes. Imām Mālik ﷻ would say: "Learn good manners before seeking knowledge."

in which they feel mocked or devalued, for God Almighty says: "Do not defame one another, nor call each other by offensive nicknames" (49:11).

Yūsuf ﷺ remained in prison for several years after his former, fellow prisoner had been 'made to forget' (12:42) to relay his name to the palace by Satan. However, the same companion finally returned to him searching for the interpretation of a strange dream the King had seen and addressed him in a dignified manner saying: "Truthful Yūsuf!" (12:46). As mentioned, Yūsuf ﷺ had already shown him and the other companion respect and honour by saying: "O my fellow prisoners", which clearly strengthened this bond between the individuals. It is important that as people of faith we make each other feel valued, and this can only be done through good manners and etiquettes. The esteemed Imām Mālik ﷺ would say: "Learn good manners before seeking knowledge", and our Prophet ﷺ said: "Nothing will be heavier on the Day of Resurrection in the scale of the believer than good manners" (Al-Tirmidhī). We sometimes underestimate the impact of a small gesture or kind act towards a fellow human being, and it can only really be appreciated when the same is done to us, especially if we are feeling down at the time.

It is in fact through our good character that true honour is attained, and this is what we see in the example of the magicians of Pharaoh when they challenged Prophet Mūsā ﷺ. This great messenger, who was from the lineage of Yaʿqūb ﷺ, was accused of being a sorcerer even after providing his

'We sometimes underestimate the impact of a small gesture or kind act towards a fellow human being, and it can only really be appreciated when the same is done to us, especially if we are feeling down at the time.

people with clear signs and evidence. Pharaoh demanded a showdown between his best magicians and Mūsā ﷺ, and before they faced off, the magicians proposed: "Moses, will you cast [your staff] first, or shall we be the first to cast?" (7:115). Mūsā ﷺ allowed them to throw first, after which we know his staff transformed into a giant serpent which stunned the onlookers. These magicians, as Allāh ﷻ tells us, fell into prostration and submitted to the Lord of Mūsā ﷺ, whilst Pharaoh and his men observed with much anger. Some commentators mention that what led to the guidance of these magicians was the small gesture they had presented to Prophet Mūsā ﷺ at the beginning. Just the act of offering Mūsā ﷺ to go first was enough to be appreciated by Allāh ﷻ that He honoured them and bestowed upon them guidance.[18]

This illustrates why it is so important to never belittle any good deed, even if it is greeting someone with a smile on your face, and why it is far more befitting for us to work on our character and hearts instead of focusing so much on our exterior appearance. Shifting the focus from wanting to meet the standards of beauty set by society to beautifying one's character to meet the standards set by our faith should be the true goal. This process of refining one's character, however, is not a short-term one. Rather, it is one that requires a lot of self-accountability, reflection and work to achieve the desired result.

---

18 Tafsīr al-Qurṭubī

23

Spiritual Seclusion

One of the aphorisms shared by Ibn 'Aṭā'illāh ﷺ, which is often overlooked by many, in his Book of Wisdoms (Kitāb al-Ḥikam) reads: "Nothing benefits the heart more than a spiritual retreat wherein it enters the domain of meditation."

When an individual takes to solitude, they not only get more time to themselves, but they also get more time with their Creator. This is of course different to cutting oneself off from society entirely, which is clearly prohibited in our religion. In a world where we are always connected, be it through social media or various other devices, we seldom get time to think and spend with ourselves. One of the benefits of disconnecting from time to time is that we get to reflect, and reflection is what is missing from many of our lives. One of the righteous once said: "Nobody would contemplate for a long time, except that they would understand. And when they understand, they would know.

And when they know, they would act upon it." There is in fact
a strong link between solitude and spirituality, seclusion and
reflection, as well as isolation and contemplation in our faith.

Yūsuf ﷺ found himself in a situation where he was
forced to spend a lot of time in isolation. Being in the prison,
he was not left with much choice. However, this was in fact
a blessing in disguise for him, as it enabled him to spend a
lot of time reflecting and contemplating. All those years in
solitude, limiting his interaction with others, prepared him
for when he would eventually leave the prison; spending
more of his time in worship and less time being distracted
increased his focus and allowed him to plan ahead for the
future, putting him in a stronger position than ever before.

The idea of seclusion is not a strange one in the Qur'ān,
in fact it is quite the contrary. Maryam (Mary), upon her
be peace, was known to seclude herself in the chamber
of the mosque to focus on her worship, and she would
receive provisions from God directly. Prophet Zakariyyā ﷺ

There is a strong link between
solitude and spirituality, seclusion
and reflection, as well as isolation
and contemplation in our faith.

Seclusion has many benefits such as inspiring creativity and enabling one to organise their thoughts. It is a wholesome experience for us, both mentally and spiritually, to allow us time to unwind and recalibrate.

(Zacharia), upon seeing this, was inspired to seclude himself and call out to his Lord in secret, through which he was granted a child in Yaḥyā ﷺ (John). Prophet Yūnus ﷺ was able to reflect in the most unusual of places, in the belly of a whale, after which he turned to Allāh ﷻ, sincerely repented and was subsequently rescued from his plight. In the Sīrah[19], seclusion became very beloved to our Prophet ﷺ especially in the years leading up to the incident of the first revelation at the age of 40.[20] He would regularly retreat to a cave on the outskirts of Makkah to reflect and contemplate, sometimes for days on end. This then led to prophethood. The common denominator here is that we should not see spending time

---

19 Biography and life of Prophet Muḥammad ﷺ
20 Ṣaḥīḥ al-Bukhārī, Book of Tafsīr

by ourselves as a bad thing, rather we should consciously prefer this at certain times so we can deeply think about our own state and devote ourselves to God without anyone there to disturb us.

Not only does seclusion allow one to reflect, but it has many other benefits such as inspiring creativity and enabling one to organise their thoughts. It is a means of *muḥāsabah* (self-accountability) by which self-awareness is attained, mistakes are rectified and spirituality is developed. It also becomes easier for one to reflect on the verses of the Qur'ān (*tadabbur*) and remind oneself of their purpose in life. Ultimately, it is a wholesome experience for us, both mentally and spiritually, as every individual needs some time to themselves every so often to unwind and recalibrate. Sometimes we end up losing someone or something in our lives and are forced to reflect during such calamities, but before that happens, we should take the initiative ourselves. Prophet Yūsuf ﷺ did not expect the turn of events that would follow in his life, however, he was now more prepared than ever to step up to deal with everything that would come his way through the will of God.

Referring to the People of Knowledge

What resulted in Yūsuf ﷺ being freed from the prison was an unexpectedly strange dream seen by the King himself. He narrates in verse 43 how he saw seven fat cows being eaten by seven lean ones, as well as seven fresh ears of grain and seven others withered. He immediately turned to his council and sought the interpretation of this dream full of ambiguities. He had never seen a dream like this, and he felt compelled to think that this was not just a random occurrence, rather there must have been a deeper, underlying reason for him to have been shown this.

The response from the King's council is worth noting. Though they admitted it sounded like a very confusing dream with different layers of ambiguity, they very quickly clarified: "We do not know the interpretation of such dreams" (12:44). This is important because they did not speak without knowledge just to please the King, which they could have done. Instead, they made their position noticeably clear. It is quite easy for one to give an opinion on a matter which they have no expertise or knowledge on, but this is not in coherence with what we are taught in the Scripture. In fact, the command in the Qur'ān is very explicit: "Ask those who have knowledge if you do not know" (16:43). If you have an enquiry, there is no harm in turning to the people of that particular field to give you an answer. In fact, we should be humble enough to say 'I don't know' and pass it on to someone more qualified to deal with it. It was known about many of the early scholars, including Imām Mālik ﷺ, that they would believe that saying 'I don't

'Referring to the people of knowledge and expertise is vital if we wânt to understand the different aspects of our faith better. It is also potentially a huge danger if one without knowledge speaks on a matter relating to Islām.

'A half-qualified doctor can, potentially put someone's life at risk, and likewise, a half-qualified or self-proclaimed scholar can, put someone's faith at risk.

know' is half of knowledge because knowledge must be approached with humility for it ultimately comes from God. Moreover, the etiquette is to frequently say 'Allāh knows best' (Allāhu a'lam), even if one knows the answer, because we may have made a mistake or misunderstood, thus covering any of our own shortcomings.

It is said that 'Alī, may God ennoble his face, was once asked a question by a man, so he gave an answer. He was then informed that his answer was wrong and was subsequently corrected. Instead of rebuking the individual or feeling ashamed, 'Alī ﷺ admitted that he was wrong, without hesitation. He then went on to quote the latter part of verse 76 from Sūrah Yūsuf: "Above those ranking in knowledge is the One All-Knowing".[21] Thus, we learn that there is always someone more knowledgeable than us and,

---

21 Tafsīr al-Ṭabarī

above all, God is All-Knowing. Referring to the people of knowledge and expertise is vital if we want to understand the different aspects of our faith better. It is also potentially a huge danger if one without knowledge speaks on a matter relating to Islām. After all, a half-qualified doctor can potentially put someone's life at risk, and likewise, a half-qualified or self-proclaimed scholar can put someone's faith at risk.

Yūsuf ﷺ's companion from prison (who had been freed) happened to hear about the King's dream after this gathering, and suddenly, after all these years, remembered his noble friend whom he spent time with. He hurried to the King and sought permission to leave, for he knew only one person who had the answer and had knowledge of dream interpretations. This companion did what needed to be done—he turned to the expert. It was through this that Yūsuf ﷺ now came back into the spotlight after many exhausting years in prison, and, at last, Allāh ﷻ presented him with the perfect opportunity to leave prison and continue his life as it once was, or perhaps with further twists in store.

25

Not Withholding a Skill or Talent

Prophet Yūsuf ﷺ was a clear person of knowledge, and it is in his dealings of dream interpretation that we are able to see the skill with which he navigated this gift that had been bestowed upon him by God.

When considering the power dynamics within a prison and amongst inmates, one of the most obvious factors is that those with something to offer others are usually at the top of the food chain. Despite Yūsuf ﷺ holding such great knowledge of dream interpretation, he neither delayed his help nor set any conditions stipulating guarantee of his release before interpreting the dream. He explained that seven consecutive years of drought would follow the seven years ahead, which would then end with a year in which rain would fall in abundance. He further offered advice on what needed to be done to overcome the drought, saying that they should store away the grain and provisions in the years ahead "except a little", which they could eat and survive on (12:47-49). His immediate interpretation was an acknowledgement of the fact that this ability to interpret dreams was a gift that was given to him by Allāh ﷻ and one that he had no need to be opportunistic with. We can draw from this that we should not withhold our skills and talents because they have been given to us for a reason. Although the reason may not seem entirely apparent at the time of discovering your talent or skill, take heart in knowing that Allāh ﷻ has endowed us with a variety of qualities so that we may be of benefit to society in some way, shape or form.

In many ways, these abilities being gifted to us as individuals is a form of sustenance (*rizq*); Allāh ﷻ has

All things are a manifestation of the intention with which they were created, and therefore it is incumbent upon us believers to utilise our personal skills and talents to be of service in the same way Prophet Yūsuf ﷺ was.

ensured we have a means of benefiting others, whilst also pleasing Him. By exercising this gift, we can use this opportunity as a way of demonstrating our *shukr* to Allāh ﷻ for securing these means for us and inspiring us to do good as "He only made an inspiration come upon you so that you would go to Him".[22] All things are a manifestation of the intention with which they were created, and therefore it is incumbent upon us believers to utilise our personal skills and talents to be of service in the same way Prophet Yūsuf ﷺ was.

Yūsuf ﷺ was eager to be in the service (*khidmah*) of others, as he explains that his gift "is from what my Lord has taught me" (12:37), and it is from this that we can take

Allāh ﷻ has taken great measure to ensure that each and every single skill or talent you possess is a reflection of your true value, but it is up to you to unlock this and unleash it into the world for the greater good.

22 Ibn ʿAṭāʾillāh, Book of Wisdoms

inspiration to be of service to others by that which has
been bestowed upon us as an honour from Al-Wahhāb, the
Supreme Bestower of Gifts. Allāh ﷻ continually bestows
gifts, favours and blessings upon all of creation, and there
is no doubt that He has given each and every single one of
His believers some kind of skill that exists for the sake of the
betterment of both ourselves and our society.

You too have been created for a purpose, with a unique
identity and set of abilities that can be utilised not only
for your own benefit, but also for the benefit of others. If
the celebrated Muslim scholars and polymaths of the past
did not realise this, we would not be benefiting from their
legacy to this day. If the most successful Muslim leaders
and thinkers did not come to terms with this, we would not
be cherishing their contributions and taking inspiration
from them even now. If the various Muslims, whose names
we aren't aware of, did not make plenty of sacrifices in the
background, we would not have made as much progress
collectively. This serves as a timely reminder that Allāh ﷻ
has taken great measure to ensure that each and every single
skill or talent you possess is a reflection of your true value,
but it is up to you to unlock this and unleash it into the
world for the greater good.

26

Opportunities in Life

As time passes, life will present you with many opportunities, and it is up to you whether you let them slip away or decide to capitalise on them. It is your choice to either disregard it or to rise to the challenge. There will be other times, however, where you will have to carve out your own opportunities. Sometimes you will have to take the initiative and make something happen yourself. All of these situations are from God, as we believe it is He who opens up pathways and doors for us. Fortunate, therefore, is the one who understands this and takes advantage of what is ahead.

For Yūsuf ﷺ, there were windows of opportunities given to him that he welcomed and made use of. The first was the opportunity to interpret the dream of the King, which he clearly relayed to the freed prisoner. The King, after hearing this interpretation, ordered the release of Yūsuf ﷺ from prison. Before leaving, Yūsuf ﷺ wanted to make certain that his integrity and honour was not to be questioned following the incident involving the Minister's wife and the other women from Egypt many years prior to his incarceration. After finally clearing his name and being told: "We know nothing indecent about him" (12:51), Yūsuf ﷺ met with the King of Egypt. Now was the chance for him to carve out an opportunity and take advantage of his presence in front of the most powerful man in the land, who was already impressed by him and was indebted to him following the interpretation of the strange dream he saw. "Put me in charge of the nation's treasures", he says in verse 55, "I am truly reliable and adept". In other words, he is affirming that he has been bestowed with the necessary knowledge to undertake this task, and he is best suited to take care of this.

The response that followed from the King was positive and, within a short space of time, Yūsuf ﷺ went from being

Life will present you with many opportunities, and it is up to you whether you let them slip away or decide to capitalise on them. It is your choice to either disregard it or to rise to the challenge.

held in the prison to now landing himself an opportunity of a lifetime, becoming the treasurer of Egypt and a newly appointed minister. The same land he was brought to with little value in the eyes of the people, was now under his authority. Allāh ﷻ informs us: "In this way, We settled Yūsuf in the land" (12:56). This was the plan of the Almighty all along, with the struggles and endurance of His beloved servant soon to pay off.

There are not many people who could stand before a king and make such a request, but Yūsuf ﷺ was an exception, for he knew he was the only one best equipped to deal with the situation at hand. The people of Egypt and

Sometimes our prayers are directly answered and an opportunity presents itself, but other times we need to have the courage to just ask or create our own opportunities, especially if we know that we can bring benefit to others.

its surrounding areas would soon suffer with the famine ahead, and with his knowledge and expertise, he would be able to take charge and help them through this. What was demonstrated by Yūsuf ﷺ when he said he was the best to take care of this role was not arrogance in the least bit, which some may wrongly assume. Rather, it was a wise move that we can all learn from. Sometimes our prayers are directly answered and an opportunity presents itself, but other times we need to have the courage to just ask or create our own opportunities, especially if we know that we can bring benefit to others. With the knowledge of dream interpretations that he was equipped with, as well as his level of integrity and trustworthiness, there was no other individual better suited for this role. God had certainly honoured Yūsuf ﷺ in this life, a man who had grown through his struggles, by granting him the honourable position as treasurer. This position was well deserved, and though he now had what many would covet—status, popularity and wealth—this did not divert his focus from his main objective in life, it did not affect his relationship and bond with his Creator. Most importantly, the worldly life did not consume his heart and allow him to lose sight of the real life—the Hereafter.

27

Jannah-Driven Mindset

We are reminded daily that this is but a temporary life and that the Hereafter is far better than that which we are experiencing right now, and yet, we often allow ourselves to be overcome with sadness and grief. But the truth is, these tests are part and parcel of reaching the Final Abode that "is better for you than the first [life]", as we are told in this beautiful verse (93:4). It can be easy to allow ourselves to think that we are the only ones enduring the struggles of this worldly life, but this verse was in fact revealed as a promise to our beloved Prophet ﷺ to console him and remind him that though times may be hard, this is not the end.

Prophet Yūsuf ﷺ is reminded throughout his life that the Eternal Abode, namely the *ākhirah*, is better for him than that which he lives through now, especially in verse 57, which is preceded by a description of Yūsuf ﷺ's worldly gains. Here, we're reminded that: "the reward of the Hereafter is far better for those who are faithful and are mindful [of God]". This verse is one that reinforces the idea that despite all the power and status that Yūsuf ﷺ was able to accumulate in his life on this earth, he was still yearning for his Lord and the home which awaits in the Hereafter. This, however, did not mean that he neglected his worldly roles and responsibilities. If anything, this desire to live the eternal life for Allāh ﷻ's sake alone seemed to inspire Yūsuf ﷺ to seek goodness and success in every way Allāh ﷻ deemed fit for him.

Like our beloved Yūsuf ﷺ and Muḥammad ﷺ, we should encourage ourselves to stay focused on attaining the best for the Hereafter through the means provided for good in this life. Ibn al-Qayyim, may Allāh ﷻ have mercy on him, describes people to be of three types in this regard.

Despite all the power and status that Yūsuf ﷺ was able to accumulate in his life on this earth, he was still yearning for his Lord and the home which awaits in the Hereafter.

'Like our beloved 'Yūsuf ﷷ and 'Muḥammad' ﷺ, we should encourage ourselves to stay focused on attaining the best for the Hereafter through the means provided for good in this life.

The first are those who do good and store their deeds for the Hereafter by ensuring all their actions are intentionally for the sake of seeking His pleasure. The second type are those who, despite having an awareness of Allāh ﷻ, work towards the worldly life with no acknowledgement that their deeds will be held to account on the Day of Recompense. And finally, the third type are those who are classified to be amongst the biggest losers both in this life and the Hereafter for they do not work for either of the worlds and simply bide their time.[23]

From amongst these three types, we should strive to be of the first kind and most like our beloved prophets throughout the history of Islām. We can do this by cultivating a 'Jannah-driven' mindset which focuses on

---

23 Ibn Qayyim al-Jawziyyah, Inner Dimensions of the Prayer

maximising our actions and intentions to be only for the
goodness of the Hereafter. There is a *du'ā* in verse 201
of Sūrah Al-Baqarah which we can implement into our
daily routine to maintain our focus, seeking success in
both worlds without losing sight of His pleasure and the
promise of His paradise: "Our Lord, grant us the good
of this world and the Hereafter, and protect us from the
torment of the Fire".

Ultimately, our existence in this life is for Allāh ﷻ, and it
is within our best interests to make an attempt at emulating
our beloved prophets before us so that we may live a life of
peace and contentment in the Eternal Abode, as is promised
to them and us. "This worldly life is no more than play and
amusement. But the Hereafter is indeed the real life, if only
they knew" (29:64).

LESSON
28

True Tawakkul

With all the unprecedented events taking place in Yūsuf ﷺ's life, hope is one thing that he held on to. His hope and trust in God guided him through; from the well, to the palace and even in the cell of the prison. In fact, if you can remember, it was revealed to him in the darkness of the well that he would one day inform his brothers of their actions while they would be unaware of who he was. Now, the time had come for another promise to be fulfilled.

Busy carrying out his duty as a treasurer in the years of famine that had struck Egypt and afflicted the masses, Yūsuf ﷺ's brothers arrived from their village to seek help for their own family. They had no idea that the Minister of the land whom they were relying on was the same vulnerable child they once tried to get rid of and left for dead. Yūsuf ﷺ recognised them immediately—ten handsome brothers as one unit, wearing familiar clothes and speaking with a distinct dialect. He did not disclose his identity to them on this occasion, though he was full of mixed emotions and certainly would have been tempted to do so. The custom was that for each person who came, they would be able to take a camel-load of provisions to help them through the days of hardship.[24] Yūsuf ﷺ, however, realised his beloved younger brother, Binyāmīn (Benjamin), was missing. Yūsuf ﷺ and Binyāmīn shared the same mother, making them full brothers, which is why they were always so close to one another. As well as this, Binyāmīn remained loyal to Yūsuf ﷺ and was never involved in any plot against him. Yūsuf ﷺ suggested to his older brothers that if they wanted another whole load, they should bring him. This was yet another intelligent move from someone who longed to be reunited with his brother and father. The brothers were determined to convince their father Yaʿqūb ﷺ, who understandably was extremely hesitant after what had once happened to Yūsuf ﷺ,

Surely Allāh loves those who put their trust in Him but Allāh ﷻ also says that He is sufficient for those who have placed their trust in Him.

24 Tafsīr Ibn Kathīr

to release Binyāmīn to their care. After taking a pledge from all his sons that they would return with no mishaps and after telling them to enter Egypt separately through "different gates", instead of as one large group, Yaʿqūb ﷺ says: "In Him I put my trust (*tawakkul*), and in Him let the faithful put their trust" (12:67).

Allāh ﷻ announces His love for the people of *tawakkul*, saying: "When you have decided on a course of action, put your trust (*tawakkul*) in God. Surely God loves those who put their trust in Him" (3:159). Not only this, but Allāh ﷻ says He is sufficient for those who have *tawakkul* in Him: "Whoever puts their trust in Allāh, then He is sufficient for them" (65:3). *Tawakkul* in Allāh ﷻ can loosely be translated as having full hope in Him or placing one's reliance in God.

Allāh ﷻ is our Wakīl, meaning we transfer responsibility to Him and Him alone to take care of us and do things in our best interests. In other words, He is our Guardian and Protector, and always has our back.

Taking from the means of this world does not negate our tawakkul. Rather, part of tawakkul is exerting our efforts then leaving the rest to Allāh ﷻ.

However, we can better understand what *tawakkul* means when we understand Allāh's name 'Al-Wakīl'. We are taught to frequently recite the following: "Allāh is sufficient for us, and He is the best Guardian" (3:173). Here, Allāh ﷻ is referred to as Al-Wakīl, which can be translated as 'The Guardian' or 'The Disposer of Affairs'. The term *wakīl* is also a legal term which refers to a power of attorney. It is someone you trust and transfer responsibility to, knowing that they will make decisions on your behalf and in your best interests. Allāh ﷻ is our Wakīl, meaning we transfer responsibility to Him and Him alone to take care of us and do things in our best interests. In other words, He is our Guardian and Protector, and always has our back.

There is a famous narration in the Sunan of Imām al-Tirmidhī in which we are told: "Tie your camel, then have tawakkul in Allāh". When the Prophet ﷺ said: "Tie your camel", we can understand this today as 'lock your car'. A person who has misunderstood *tawakkul* will park

The true meaning of tawakkul is that we do whatever we can and then leave the rest to Allāh. Even if something were to happen, we can still find solace in knowing that we did what we could and that the rest was up to the decree of God Almighty.

their vehicle, leave their windows down, have valuable belongings on display and not lock their car. They will say that Allāh ﷻ will look after the car and them, and that there is really nothing to worry about. Such individuals don't actually have *tawakkul*, instead they have something called *'tamannī'*, which is to have false hopes in Allāh ﷻ. The true meaning of *tawakkul* is that we do whatever we can and then leave the rest to Allāh ﷻ. In other words, we put our windows up, take the valuable belongings with us, lock our cars and then trust that Allāh ﷻ will take care of it for us. Even if something were to happen, we can still find solace in knowing that we did what we could and that the rest was up to the decree (*qadr*) of God Almighty.

Taking from the means of this world does not negate our *tawakkul*. Rather, part of tawakkul is exerting our efforts then leaving the rest to Allāh ☙. This is found in the example of Prophet Yaʿqūb ☙, who after taking the pledge from his sons and asking them to enter Egypt separately from different gates, then leaves the rest to Allāh ☙. By doing so, he wanted to ward off any harm from these eleven handsome men who would have been travelling collectively. He did what was in his capacity at the time, but then knew that the rest was out of his hands. Prophet Yūsuf ☙ did the same, as he made the necessary moves to be reunited with his family then had *tawakkul* in God. Indeed, *tawakkul* is an integral part of our faith, and correctly understanding and applying it is what helps us navigate and get through life under the supervision of our Guardian.

29

Avoiding Ḥastiness

With the fast-paced lives that many of us live today, it is easy to outpace yourself and make hasty decisions in the mix of it all. We live in a world that teaches us to constantly keep up and be decisive, yet we often mistake this for becoming hasty in our affairs. God tells us that: "Humankind is made of haste (*'ajal*)" (21:37), and our Prophet ﷺ taught us: "Hastiness (*'ajalah*) is from the Shayṭān" (Al-Tirmidhī). It is not from the innate quality of a believer that they should be hasty, rather they are by nature calm and composed in every situation.

Throughout the story of Prophet Yūsuf ﷺ, we find him to be composed and patient in the face of many trials and tribulations. This was no easy feat for him however, and it is quite amazing how he maintained this attitude throughout, despite the circumstances. For example, when the King's messenger and former prisoner came to release Yūsuf ﷺ from prison and take him to the King, Yūsuf ﷺ

told him: "Return to your master and ask him about the case of those women who cut their hands" (12:50). Eager to clear his name of the accused crimes, Yūsuf ﷺ delayed his release from prison even though these matters could have been resolved later. Prophet Muḥammad ﷺ even commented on this saying: "Had I stayed in prison as long as Yūsuf stayed and then the messenger came, I would have responded to his call!"[25], which goes to show that even our Prophet ﷺ praised the composure and patience of Yūsuf ﷺ. He admitted that many of us would not have been as level-headed as he was if we were to find ourselves in a similar situation.

'Even 'Prophet 'Muḥammad ﷺ praised the amazing composure and patience of 'Yūsuf ﷺ. He admitted that many of us would not have been as level-headed as he was if we were to find ourselves in a similar situation.

---

25 Ṣaḥīḥ al-Bukhārī, Book of Dream Interpretations

The same is seen when Yūsuf ﷺ first recognises his brothers as they entered Egypt. After years of heartbreak and separation, which no doubt they were guilty of causing, he could have immediately taken them to account for abandoning him in the well and exercised the authority he had in the land. However, he waited until the right moment to reveal his real identity and dealt with them in an excellent manner, which required wisdom and forbearance. He sent his brothers back after having returned their goods to them in the hope that they would bring his younger brother Binyāmīn on the following occasion. This move certainly paid off, and Binyāmīn was now reunited with his dear brother after many years of grief. There are many other examples of Yūsuf ﷺ's composure in this story, all of which teach us how to respond amidst the turbulence we often face in our lives.

'When we have to decide between what is right and wrong, Satan knows we will most likely opt for the short-term pleasures. This is why it is so important to take things easy in life and avoid hastiness at all costs.

A lack of hastiness requires us to think more long-term. We end up being forced to think about the consequences of our actions and decisions, which in turn helps filter out the ones that won't benefit us or could potentially cause us and others harm. That is not to say that we allow a sense of indecisiveness to cripple us, it just means that we don't do things we'll live to regret. If hastiness is indeed from Satan, as our Prophet ﷺ warned us, then why is that the case? When we're going through some hardship, he knows we will end up losing patience and hope in God quicker than others. When we find ourselves in a disagreement with someone, he knows we will be quick to lose our temper and lash out. When we have to decide between what is right and wrong, he knows we will most likely opt for the short-term pleasures. This is why it is so important to take things easy in life and avoid hastiness at all costs. As the famous saying in Arabic goes: 'In calmness there is peace (*salāmah*), and in hastiness there is regret (*nadāmah*)'.

Suppressing Your Anger

An integral part of remaining calm and not being hasty is to suppress your anger in the heat of the moment. Allāh Almighty promises an entire Garden of Paradise to the *Muttaqīn* (People of *taqwā*), who are those "who give in prosperity and adversity, who restrain their anger and pardon others. God loves those who do good" (3:134).

The people of excellence are the *Muḥsinīn*—those who possess such aforementioned qualities and are in the habit of performing good deeds. You may recall that it was Prophet Yūsuf ﷺ who was described as being from amongst the *Muḥsinīn* in some of the previous verses, and one of his distinct qualities was that he was able to control his anger, even when he was pushed to the limit.

Yūsuf ﷺ was finally able to embrace his brother
Binyāmīn for the first time after many long years, but
he had to find a way of keeping him in Egypt by making
his penultimate move. He secretly had a valuable item
belonging to the King placed in Binyāmīn's bag before he
left. The law at the time dictated that the one found guilty
of stealing would be handed over to the victim of the theft
as a slave, meaning that Binyāmīn would be handed over to
Yūsuf ﷺ—which is exactly what he wanted.

The rest of the brothers, shocked by what Binyāmīn
had done, now faced a dilemma. They knew that if they
returned to their father without him, this would raise further
suspicions and completely break his heart following what
had already happened to Yūsuf ﷺ many years before. At
the same time, they could not defend their brother for the
supposed crime he had committed. As their frustrations built,
they exclaimed: "If he has stolen, so did his [full] brother
before him" (12:77). The brothers were of course referring to
Yūsuf ﷺ, accusing him also of supposedly stealing as a child
and bringing up the past in an unpleasant manner. This no
doubt hurt Yūsuf ﷺ, especially after having been so kind
towards them in his treatment, despite what they had done.
The Qur'ān narrates: "But Yūsuf kept it within himself and
did not reveal anything to them. And said [to himself]: 'You
are in a far worse situation. God knows best [the truth of]
what you claim'" (12:77). It is amazing how Yūsuf ﷺ was
able to keep himself composed at this point, and what is even

more amazing is how he was not just standing there as an oppressed younger brother of theirs, but as one of the most powerful men of the land who had the ability to respond and retaliate as he pleased. Indeed, it takes a truly strong person to be able to suppress their rage, as our Prophet ﷺ said: "The strong one is he who controls himself at the time of anger".[26]

When we usually describe the process of anger building up, we say that our 'blood is boiling'. There is in fact an explanation for this provided by our Prophet ﷺ in a famous narration: "The Shaytān runs in humans like the flowing of blood".[27] What this shows is that it is in fact Satan's influence running deep within us, inciting us to unleash the rage that has built up so we can cause as much damage as possible. This is where self-control is vital, yet it is probably one of the most difficult things to do.

We are taught by our Prophet ﷺ: "When one of you becomes angry, let them remain silent" (Musnad Aḥmad). We should consciously make the effort to not speak and let ourselves cool off. Usually, the words that come out from our mouths in this state are in the form of expletives or harsh statements. We end up realising the severity of our words afterwards, and even if we did not intend to hurt anyone by them, like bullets, they cannot be taken back.

---

26 Ṣaḥīḥ al-Bukhārī, Book of Adab
27 Ṣaḥīḥ Muslim, Book of Greetings

Another practical form of guidance from the Sunnah is that if someone is standing, they should sit down. If they are sitting, they should lie down.[28] Other narrations mention you should leave the place you are in entirely and go elsewhere. This is to limit one's movement and interactions, as someone sitting or lying down cannot retaliate like the one who is standing. These prophetic teachings on anger management are most definitely effective and help one to suppress the rage that burns within them at critical moments.

It is thus apparent why Allāh ﷻ, the Lord of Mercy, promises such a vast reward for those who control their anger, and why our Prophet ﷺ emphasised this a great deal in his advice to his companions. The righteous are known to not only be fair people, but individuals who are understanding and forgiving. They are those who receive mercy from Allāh ﷻ and extend their mercy towards others. Anger is a natural emotion no doubt, and at times it can even be justified to show it. However, the righteous are those who are masters of self-control. They love and despise for God's sake alone.

---

28 Sunan Abī Dāwūd, Book of Adab

31

Displaying Emotions

L ove. Anger. Sadness. This story covers an entire spectrum of emotions which sums up what we tend to experience in our lives. The question then arises, to what extent can we display these emotions, and in particular, sadness? Does the fact that we are feeling emotionally low necessarily reflect our spiritual state?

When the brothers returned to their father without Binyāmīn, Yaʿqūb ﷺ was informed about yet another loss and he could not help but think this was extremely suspicious behaviour on account of his sons. He exclaimed: "No! Your souls have prompted you to do wrong" (12:83), before uttering the words "a beautiful patience" once again as he consoled himself through the despair. Allāh ﷻ then details in verse 84 the true extent of what he had been going through: "He turned away from them, saying, 'Alas for Joseph!', and his eyes turned white out of the grief he suppressed."

In this day and age, it is not uncommon to hear statements such as 'real men don't cry', or at least there is a culture of masking one's emotions. Here we have a man, who is also a prophet sent by God, not only displaying his emotions but losing his eyesight due to excessive weeping! This grief Ya'qūb ﷺ was experiencing is described as "*ḥuzn*" in the Qur'ān. Our Prophet ﷺ would in fact seek refuge in God from two things in particular: *hamm* and *ḥuzn*.[29] These two words denote a feeling of sadness; *hamm* being an anxiety over what is to come in the future and *ḥuzn* being an overwhelming grief from a past experience. Even after all these years, Ya'qūb ﷺ was still grieving over Yūsuf ﷺ and was unapologetic about it, yet those around him could not understand this. "They said: 'By God! You will ruin your health if you do not stop thinking of Yūsuf, or even die'" (12:85).

Our Prophet ﷺ taught us that shedding tears is a display of mercy and affection granted to us by God. He explicitly stated that he was grieved by his son's departure and he was experiencing ḥuzn.

---

29 Ṣaḥīḥ al-Bukhārī, Book of Invocations

Displaying emotions when going through a difficulty by no means indicates any deficiencies in one's spirituality, nor does it negate one's connection with God. Rather, it is a means of drawing closer to Him by responding to the test as a believer should.

This is no different to the example of Prophet Muḥ ammad ﷺ, who himself suffered many losses, burying most of his sons and daughters during his lifetime. When his beloved son, Ibrāhīm ؏, was breathing his last breath, the Prophet ﷺ's eyes welled up with tears and he began to cry. Some of the companions, including ʿAbd al-Raḥmān Ibn ʿAwf, were surprised by this and asked: "O Messenger of Allāh, you too weep?", to which he responded: "It is mercy". The famous statement then followed: "The eyes are shedding tears and the heart is grieved, and we will not say except what pleases our Lord. O Ibrāhīm! Indeed, we are grieved by your departure."[30]

---

30 Ṣaḥīḥ al-Bukhārī, Book of Funerals

Our Prophet ﷺ taught us that shedding tears is a display of mercy and affection granted to us by God. He explicitly stated that he was grieved by his son's departure and that he was indeed experiencing *huzn* at this point. The best of examples is acknowledging that this is completely natural and that we should not feel ashamed in displaying our emotions when going through a difficulty. This by no means indicates any deficiencies in one's spirituality, nor does it negate one's connection with God. Rather, it is a means of drawing closer to Him by responding to this test as a believer should. Moreover, it restores one's emotional balance and helps one to recover from grief. Bottling one's emotions has many mental and spiritual harms, but by following the examples set by Prophet Ya'qūb and Prophet Muḥammad, may Allāh's peace and blessings be upon them, we will be able to continuously flourish and grow, both emotionally and spiritually.

Complaining to Allāh

We have learned that the most beautiful type of patience is one in which there is contentment with God's decree and a lack of complaint to others. It has also been clarified that it is very natural to feel and display human emotions, and that there sometimes needs to be an outlet for this. Therefore, Prophet Yaʿqūb ﷺ, at this current time of distress, said: "I complain of my grief and sorrow only to Allāh" (12:86).

There is a fundamental difference between complaining *about* Allāh ﷻ and complaining *to* Allāh ﷻ. To complain about Allāh ﷻ is to question His decree and show signs of discontent, but to complain to Him is to do what is encouraged of us, especially in times of adversity. It is to pour our hearts out to the Almighty through prayer, detailing the nature of the adversity we are experiencing and beseeching Him for His help and comfort. This is precisely what Yaʿqūb ﷺ did when he faced this new trial, realising that complaining to others would be of no avail, but complaining to Allāh 🕮 would be the solution. After all, his own sons had let him down on more than one occasion, and he was now at a frail age with little or no sight, so he knew it was only Allāh 🕮 he could turn towards.

In the Sīrah, we find a similar stance taken by our Prophet 🕮 after he went to the people of Ṭā'if to invite them to Islām. He was met with much hostility and was driven out by the locals. Our Beloved 🕮 had stones thrown at him by them, and he left with blood dripping from his blessed body. In a state of shock and grief, he called out: "O Allāh, to You I complain…" and made *du'ā* thereafter.[31] "O Allāh, I complain to You" were also the words of the great companion of the Prophet 🕮, Khawlah Bint Tha'labah, whose husband declared a pre-Islamic form of divorce (*zihār*) on her. Her complaint was such that God Himself revealed a chapter in the Qur'ān titled 'Al-Mujādilah', referring to this woman who argued her case, and began with: "God has certainly heard the words of the woman who pleaded with you (Prophet) concerning her husband and complained to God, and God has heard your exchange…" (58:1). How amazing is it that not only did God acknowledge her complaint, but He registered it for eternity in the Qur'ān by responding through revelation!

The examples provided are sufficient to highlight how widely this was practiced by some of the best people to walk

---

31 Sīrah Ibn Hishām and Tārīkh al-Ṭabarī

this earth. One who is distressed will naturally call out and complain to The Most High, as Allāh ﷻ says: "Who is it that answers the distressed when they call upon Him and removes their suffering?" (27:62). This shows that harm will actually be removed, and obstacles can be overcome if we call upon our Lord in this manner.

Many of us may not be aware of how therapeutic simply engaging in *duʿā* can be and the benefits of it, both spiritually and mentally. It is not just a form of asking, but it is also a form of conversing with God and offloading what is on your mind and heart. One can complain to Him about what they are going through, articulate exactly how they are feeling and seek aid from Him—the only One who can ultimately rescue you. Perhaps one may argue that God already knows how we are feeling and what we are facing thus there is no need for us to break things down in such a manner, and though this is true, it is from the etiquette of *duʿā* that one humbles themselves before the Almighty and seeks His assistance regardless. It is also encouraged that we make our

To complain to Allāh ﷻ is to pour our hearts out to Him through prayer beseeching Him for His help and comfort.

voices more 'familiar' to Him. That is not to say that God doesn't know of our existence or that which troubles us—He is our Creator and His knowledge encompasses all things—but there is an effort required on our end to build a stronger relationship between us, the servants, and God, the Master.

An example we can perhaps relate to is a friend who calls us every so often only to ask for favours. They make no effort beyond that to keep in touch or to build a friendship, but they come to you with the sole purpose of taking and not giving. Though you may accommodate on a few occasions, it will naturally come to a point where your frustrations outweigh your generosity, and you subsequently deny them the chance to ask again. If on the other hand, however, they made an effort to communicate and make time for you, you would have no issue with helping out a close friend who would likely do the same for you. Now understand, albeit in a different context, how it looks when we only make *du'ā* and turn to Allāh ﷻ at our times of need and do nothing else beyond that. Would our voices be familiar to Him, as was the voice of Prophet Yūnus ﷺ when he called out from the belly of the whale? This is certainly a point to reflect on, whereby we ensure we are consistent in this regard and make an effort throughout to connect with God. Prophet Yūsuf ﷺ and Prophet Yaʿqūb ﷺ were from amongst those who continuously called out and remembered their Lord in times of ease and difficulty, which is what helped them remain hugely optimistic at moments of extreme uncertainty.

Having an Optimistic Outlook

Undoubtedly, it is easy to become a pessimist when experiencing the more adverse conditions of life. At that point, it seems as if things will never improve and that there is no way out. The believers are encouraged by God Almighty to be a people of optimism, and it is in fact from the Sunnah to remain optimistic at all times.

After Binyāmīn was ordered to remain in Egypt, the eldest brother of Yūsuf ﷺ took it upon himself to desperately make things right for the sake of his father Yaʿqūb ﷺ, knowing full well how pressing the situation was. He said to the rest of his brothers: "Do you not remember that your father took a solemn pledge from you in the name of God and before that you failed in your duty with regard to Yūsuf? I will not leave this land until my father gives me leave or God decides for me" (12:80). Thus, he and

Binyāmīn stayed behind, leaving his father with a gaping hole in his heart and his home, which was once filled with the joy brought to him by his twelve sons. But amidst these overshadowing events there still seemed to be a glimmer of hope for Yaʿqūb ﷺ. Exclaiming: "Perhaps Allāh will bring them all back to me…" (12:83), Yaʿqūb ﷺ did not allow the unfortunate circumstances of his life to deter him from remaining optimistic. His optimism dominated any other feeling he may have had, and this is precisely what inspired his final move. He had a strong feeling that all was not as it seemed, and that these events could not just be merely a coincidence, so he instructed: "O my sons, go and seek news of Yūsuf and his brother and do not despair of God's relief— for no one loses hope in God's relief except the disbelievers" (12:87). These words ignited something in the hearts of his sons, and they immediately made their way to Egypt once more, with relief from Allāh ﷻ awaiting them.

> ʿYaʿqūb ﷺ did not allow the unfortunate circumstances of his life to deter him from remaining optimistic. His optimism dominated any other feeling he may have had.

The believers are always optimistic and never despair because they are able to hold on to something so dear that sets them apart from the rest—their faith and submission to God.

The word in Arabic used for relief in this verse is *"rawḥ"* which literally comes from the word used to describe a breeze or wind *(rīḥ)*. In the hot climate of the desert, the Arabs would find nothing more relieving and relaxing for them than a gentle breeze to cool them down. Just like the one who traverses the tough conditions of the desert, we all traverse our own paths in life, and from time to time we are provided with a relief from God which helps us continue our respective journeys. What Yaʿqūb ﷺ also taught his sons was to not lose hope nor become despondent, for this relief was almost certain to come.

Even our Prophet Muḥammad ﷺ would say that he loved words of optimism,[32] and he was always able to maintain a positive approach to the different situations he would find

---

32 Ṣaḥīḥ Muslim, Book of Greetings

himself in. He taught us to never believe in bad omens nor to uphold a pessimistic outlook on things. This optimism was in fact contagious—even his companions maintained this in the most testing of times. During the Battle of the Trench, where the Muslims found themselves up against an army of 10,000 strong, soon to be allied with another Jewish tribe who would break the peace treaty between them, they did not lose hope at a time when most people would have. In the Qur'ān, Allāh ﷻ describes how they reacted when they saw the confederates approaching: "This only served to increase their faith and submission [to God]" (33:22). The believers were no doubt slightly shaken by this initially, but they did not stumble and kept their faith strong. Contrastingly, the onlooking hypocrites reacted by saying: "God and His Messenger promised us nothing but delusions" (33:12). This summarises exactly what was meant by the conclusion of verse 87 of Sūrah Yūsuf: "No one loses hope in God's relief except the disbelievers". The believers are always optimistic and never despair because they are able to hold on to something so dear that sets them apart from the rest—their faith in God and submission to Him. When we wonder when the relief and divine aid from God will arrive, we should remember: "Unquestionably, the help of Allāh is near" (2:214)

34

Accepting Your Flaws

Perhaps one of the most difficult things we can do is to acknowledge our faults and mistakes. We are all flawed in our own ways, but to muster up the courage to admit this can be quite daunting at times. Our egos do not thrive on us apologising or on our willingness to change because it can make us vulnerable in the sight of others.

We may wonder if the brothers of Yūsuf ﷺ had changed since the incident involving them and their younger sibling many years ago. As time had passed, did they now come to a realisation about their previous mistakes? Were they aware of the consequences of their actions?

The remaining sons of Yaʿqūb ﷺ, upon the request of their father, made their way back to Egypt for a final showdown with Yūsuf ﷺ. They were still not aware at this point that the Minister of the land was indeed their own brother. None but Binyāmīn, who was reunited with his beloved brother, had knowledge of this. Upon their arrival, in a desperate last attempt, they cried out: "Mighty Governor! Misfortune has afflicted us and our family. We have brought only a little merchandise but give us full measure. Be charitable to us, God rewards the charitable" (12:88). It is difficult to imagine what Yūsuf ﷺ would have been feeling at this point. He would have taken no joy in seeing his own family members in such a state of despair, even calling on him to be generous to them. Yūsuf ﷺ had been extremely patient up until this point, but this seemed to be the final straw for him too. Some of the commentators of the Qur'ān mention how Yaʿqūb ﷺ had also sent a letter with his sons, detailing how he was from a line of God's messengers who had been severely tested and how his son Binyāmīn was nothing but innocent.[33] As the emotions rushed through Yūsuf ﷺ upon reading this letter and seeing his family in such a state, he decided it was time to reveal his identity: "Do you now realise what you did to Yūsuf and his brother when you were ignorant?" (12:89). The brothers were in shock—could it be that the Minister they were addressing was in reality their dear brother? They asked: "Are you really Yūsuf?", and the response they received clarified everything: "I am Yūsuf, and this is my brother. God has been gracious to us" (12:90).

If we pause for a moment, we can reflect on this bittersweet family reunion between Yūsuf ﷺ and his

---

33 Tafsīr al-Qurṭubī

brothers. Years of patience and perseverance were invested into making this meeting happen. It was as if Yūsuf ﷺ could see flashbacks of the terrifying moment he was cast into the depths of the well and how he was reassured through divine inspiration that this moment would come. A moment where he would inform his brothers about what they had done but they would not even recognise him. It probably did not make much sense to Yūsuf ﷺ then, but it certainly did now! God never fails in His promise, and better days certainly lie ahead.

From the perspective of his brothers, they too would have experienced flashbacks of their own. The times when they defied their father, a prophet of God, and thought that they knew better than him. The grim moment when they hatched their plan collectively. The merciless attempt to permanently get rid of their own kin. After that, they were simply caught in a web of lies and a lifetime of guilt. The dynamics of their household had changed, their father was left devastated

'We may be accustomed to hearing that people can never change, but if one is sincere in their approach, what's to stop them from a transformation?

and they had achieved nothing but a huge burden to carry with them wherever they went. Having reached this point however, they were determined not to repeat their mistakes: "By God! God really did favour you over all of us!", they said. They immediately acknowledged that if God had favoured someone, then it did not matter how much older or stronger than them they were. They ended their statement by admitting: "We were indeed in the wrong" (12:91).

We may be accustomed to hearing that people can never change, but if one is sincere in their approach, what's to stop them from a transformation? The brothers of Yūsuf ﷺ demonstrated that they were able to admit their faults and seek forgiveness in a dignified manner. It is essential that we learn from this—no matter how big of a crime is committed, we can always change and move on from that. That is not to say there will not be repercussions along the way or even a price to pay, but that should not deter us from embracing the light after the darkness. Yūsuf ﷺ's brothers admitted that they were wrong without offering any excuses. We are taught by our Prophet ﷺ that we are all excessive sinners, but the best of us are those who repent (Ibn Mājah). It goes without saying that you must be the bigger person to accept fault and apologise, which is precisely what the brothers did. It is also worth noting that it takes even more courage and humility to forgive after so much pain was inflicted on you, and this is the lesson we can learn from Prophet Yūsuf, may God's peace be upon him, in his amazing response that followed.

A Sincere Forgiveness

To be forgiving and tolerant of others is a trait that is deemed praiseworthy in our faith. It can be difficult to pardon someone after they have wronged you, as the prospect of dismissing them is usually easier and more appealing at the time, especially when you feel hurt by their actions. Naturally, we may often become upset and displeased, and we are permitted to cool off for some time, even if it means having our own space for that duration. However, the general emphasis is on eventually forgiving and overlooking the mistake. We are all bound to make mistakes from time to time, so would we not expect others to pardon us when we do?

The brothers of Yūsuf ﷺ had now sought forgiveness from him after learning of his identity and admitted to their past faults in his presence. It was now up to Yūsuf ﷺ to either forgive them following years of heartbreak and sorrow, or to hold them to account first, which he was more than entitled to do. Nothing could undo the hurt and grief caused by them, but Yūsuf 🕊 knew that holding on to this would not make things any better, nor would it improve the situation. Life is too short, and he wanted to move past this to emphasise his desire to bring his family back together again. Without any hesitation, Yūsuf 🕊 elegantly responded to his brothers by saying: "There is no reproach on you today. May God forgive you! He is the Most Merciful of the merciful" (12:92).

This was a beautiful response from an amazing man. He attached no blame to them and understood that even the best of people can slip up from time to time. He wanted no ill feelings between him and his siblings, and this is exemplified in verse 100 when he looks back at how Allāh 🕮 had blessed him and says: "Satan sowed discord between me and my brothers". Here, Yūsuf 🕊 is freeing his brothers from any malicious intent and is instead attributing it all to Satan. With these gracious words, the brothers of Yūsuf 🕊 could now see why Allāh 🕮 had favoured him over them and why he deserved to be in the position he was. But there was no time to dwell on this and rejoice just yet, as Ya'qūb 🕊 was still at home anxiously

'Nothing could undo the hurt and grief caused onto 'Yūsuf 🕊 but he knew that holding on to it would not improve the situation.

awaiting the news. "Take this shirt of mine and lay it over my father's face", Yūsuf ﷺ said, "He will recover his sight. Then bring your whole family back to me" (12:93).

"There is no reproach on you today" were the same words echoed by our Prophet ﷺ on the day the Muslims conquered Makkah. Returning to the land he and his companions were driven out from, he forgave his people and entered the holy city peacefully.[34] Elsewhere, ʿĀʾisha ﷺ, the Mother of the Believers, was slandered against. This fabrication became widespread throughout Madinah, until it reached the ears of our Beloved ﷺ and his father in-law and blessed companion Abū Bakr ﷺ. Initiated by the hypocrites intending to cause harm to the Prophet ﷺ and his family, the false report became the news of the town very quickly, until even some of the companions themselves started to report it with their tongues. It so happened that one of the companions who became involved in the slander was Misṭaḥ ﷺ, the nephew of Abū Bakr ﷺ himself. Abū Bakr ﷺ had already been aiding his nephew financially for some time due to his struggles, so this, coupled with the fact that he was a blood relative, caused him to become extremely upset. By the time the Quranic verses were revealed to clear our mother's name and to not only restore her honour, but to elevate it, Abū Bakr ﷺ had already vowed never to provide for his nephew Misṭaḥ ﷺ again and had no intention of pardoning him. One cannot imagine the hurt a father would feel hearing such lies made against his beloved daughter and the embarrassment it would cause considering she was also from the family of the Messenger of Allāh ﷺ. Despite all this, Allāh ﷻ sent down divine guidance directly relating to this incident: "And let not those who have been graced with virtue and affluence swear to suspend donations to their kinsmen, the poor and those who emigrated in God's way. Let them pardon and forgive. Do you not wish that God should forgive you? God is Most Forgiving and Merciful" (24:22).

It is reported that upon hearing these words Abū Bakr ؓ immediately cried out: "By God, we undoubtedly wish for God to forgive us!", and he retracted his statement and pardoned Misṭaḥ ؓ.[35] Following this, he continued to provide for his nephew, who was a poor emigrant heavily relying on this aid. What a powerful example! Just like Yūsuf ؒ was able to forgive his brothers even though they plotted against him, and Abū Bakr ؓ was able to forgive his nephew despite the fact that he was involved in the slander against his daughter, we too should be able to harness the power of forgiveness if we are approached genuinely. After all, do we not expect Allāh ﷻ to forgive us and shower us with His mercy when we turn back to Him? So, why do we not then extend our mercy to others and forgive their mistakes and shortcomings? We ask Allāh ﷻ to grant us the strength and courage to forgive.

---

35 Tafsīr al-Ṭabarī

LESSON

36

The Power of Supplication

‘Ít was truly miraculous how, through the permission of Allāh ☝, Yaʻqūb ☝'s sight would be restored through the shirt of Yūsuf ☝. It was perhaps even more miraculous how Yaʻqūb ☝ was able to get a "sense of the smell of Yūsuf" (12:94) from it as the caravan departed from Egypt. One can also argue that the true miracle in this series of events was Yūsuf ☝'s ability to forgive and the sincerity of it.

When the remaining sons of Yaʻqūb ☝ returned home with the good news, they knew what they had to do first. Having sought forgiveness from their brother, they now braced themselves for a meeting with their father in which they had to admit their faults and seek forgiveness from him. By this point, Yaʻqūb ☝ had grown old, his heart had been broken over and over again and his eyesight had completely deteriorated. However, the ink had not yet dried on this spectacular story and there was still room for a happy ending! The sons cried out: "Father, ask God to forgive our sins—we were truly in the wrong!" (12:97). To which Ya'qūb ﷺ responded: "I shall ask my Lord to forgive you. He is the Most Forgiving, the Most Merciful" (12:98).

The question now arises, why did Prophet Ya'qūb ﷺ not forgive his sons at that very moment? Instead, why did he say that he would, in the near future, ask God to forgive them? Some of the commentators of the Qur'ān discuss this point, highlighting the wisdom behind his response. It is said that Ya'qūb ﷺ wanted to wait until night-time, or the last portion of the night, to make this du'ā and seek forgiveness for his sons.[36] This is because in these hours of darkness, in which most of the people are asleep, it is far more effective to offer prayers and make supplications. We learn this from our Prophet ﷺ when he was asked about the time of the greatest response for du'ā: "In the last part of the night and after the conclusion of the obligatory prayers."[37] We also learn from another narration that he ﷺ said: "The closest the Lord is to a worshipper is during the last part of the night, so if you are able to be of those who remember Allāh during that time, then do so."[38]

---

36 Tafsīr al-Baghawī
37 Jāmi' al-Tirmidhī, Book of Supplications
38 Jāmi' al-Tirmidhī, Book of Supplications

Do we really want it bad enough if we are not waking up in the middle of the night for it? Many of us claim that we have made the sufficient effort required of us, but have we forsaken our beds to offer such prayers? An employee will put in extra hours, be in the office when everyone else has gone home and sacrifice their sleep just for the sake of a promotion or pay-rise from their employer. Are we then, as servants of God, putting in the extra hours and working overtime for the sake of our Master and the Lord of the worlds? Prophet Ya'qūb ﷺ was so sincere in his forgiveness that he wanted it to be done at the best of times where there would be no question of its effectiveness. This is precisely why one of the great scholars once said: "The *du'ā* made at the dead of night is like an arrow which never misses its target."

Even generally speaking, making *du'ā* at any given point is something we should relish and make use of every single day. We should beseech God for His forgiveness, mercy and blessings; we should ask Him to alleviate any pain, suffering or difficulty we are experiencing; we should supplicate for others and ask for the goodness of both worlds. Overall, *du'ā* is an opportunity for one to connect with Allāh ﷻ in a way that is not possible through any other means. It is a chance to have a one-to-one conversation with The Most High, with no barriers in between. Allāh ﷻ Himself removed these barriers as we are told in His statement: "When My servants ask you (Prophet) about Me, I am truly near. I respond to the prayers of those who call Me, so let them respond to Me, and believe in Me, so that they may be guided" (2:186).

In this verse, Allāh ﷻ did not command the Prophet ﷺ to tell us that He is near, nor did he use the imperative 'say'. Rather, he directly informs us that He is there for His servants and promises to respond to us if we take the step to call upon Him first. We will never be left empty-handed, as our Prophet ﷺ teaches us: "Your Lord is Modest and Most Generous. He shies away from returning the hands of His servant empty when he raises them to Him."³⁹ *Duʿā* is the most flexible act of worship—we can make it at any time, in any place and in any language. Just like Allāh ﷻ responded to Prophet Yūnus ﷺ in the belly of the whale, and Prophet Ibrāhīm ﷺ in the fire, and Prophet Zakariyyā ﷺ in the chamber, He too can answer your call if you earnestly and sincerely turn to Him. Prophet Yaʿqūb ﷺ understood this, which is why he turned to Allāh ﷻ to seek forgiveness on behalf of his sons at the best of times. He had been making plenty of *duʿā* over the years, and Allāh ﷻ had finally answered his prayers. With his eyesight now restored, Yaʿqūb ﷺ prepared to travel with his family to lay his eyes on his beloved Yūsuf ﷺ once again. The time had come for the much-anticipated reunion.

---

39 Jāmiʿ al-Tirmidhi, Book of Supplications

Always Invoke Allāh's Name

Everything happens with the permission of God and everything happens by His decree. Not a day can go by without mentioning His name, as we utter it with every movement made in our prayers and even before we partake in the food we eat. We are taught to praise Him as soon as we rise from our sleep each morning and to even exalt His name before we set off on a journey. In the Qur'ān we are reminded that if we remember God, He will remember us.[40]

We often invoke His name when we are planning on doing something by saying *'in shā Allāh'*, which can be translated as 'God willing' or 'if God wills'. This is in adherence to the teachings of our faith since we rely solely on Him and leave our future to the Almighty. The correct etiquette is to say

---

40 Qur'ān, 2:152

this even if we are certain of something happening, just as Prophet Yūsuf 🕮 did when he finally welcomed his family as they were entering Egypt. Highlighted in verse 99, he says: "Enter Egypt, God willing, safely", after having welcomed them to what was to be their new home. What an amazing scene this must have been as the blessed family embraced once again and put all their troubles behind them at last!

Just like Yūsuf 🕮 added 'God willing' to his words at the arrival of his family, even though they had already reached the border and were certain to enter Egypt, we too should frequently invoke God's name with every decision and action we make. The term 'in shā Allāh' is not correctly applied in many cases, and nowadays it is often used as a replacement for 'I'm not sure', intending a 'no' or it is discarded completely if we have full certainty of something materialising. When used in a case of uncertainty, we should bear in mind that though everything does happen by God's decree, we still have to do what we can on our end. Some effort is required on our part, so it is not enough to simply say 'God willing' with hope that something can miraculously happen. We cannot forget that Prophet Yūsuf 🕮 made this statement after he had made all the necessary preparations and arrangements for his family to arrive safely in Egypt. With the case of intending a 'no', it is as if 'God willing' becomes a free pass to make ourselves feel better about kindly rejecting a request or dodging a situation. It goes without saying that we cannot invoke God's name in vain, and we should learn how to approach things in the correct manner while upholding honesty and politeness. As for the case of certainty, it has already been clarified that regardless of how sure we are of something happening, there is still great benefit in saying 'God willing' because we attribute everything to Him.

The most righteous of people are quoted to have taken God's name in the most befitting manner in different scenarios and situations. When Prophet Ibrāhīm ﷺ informed his son Prophet Ismāʿīl ﷺ (Ishmael) of the famous dream in which he saw himself sacrificing him, the response was fascinating: "My dear father, do as you are commanded and, God willing, you will find me to be of the patient."[41] When Prophet Mūsā ﷺ requested permission from his mentor Al-Khiḍr ﷺ to accompany him on the journey, he was told that he may not have what it takes, to which he responded: "God willing, you will find me patient. I will not disobey you in any way."[42] Likewise, this same prophet, when meeting the man from Madyan (Midian) who wanted to marry his daughter to him, was told: "I do not intend to make things difficult for you. God willing, you will find I am a fair man."[43]

Perhaps the most famous example of the disadvantage of not saying 'God willing' is found in the life of the Prophet

---

41 Qurʾān, 37:102
42 Qurʾān, 18:69
43 Qurʾān, 28:27

Muḥammad 鬱. As advances from the Pagan leaders of
Makkah increased and intensified, a few of them set off
to meet some of the leading Jewish scholars who had
knowledge of their scripture, in order to test the soundness
of Muḥammad 鬱's prophethood. This was no doubt an
attempt to humiliate the Messenger of Allāh 鬱, so they
returned with three questions and posed them to him.[44] The
Prophet 鬱 informed them that he would present the answer
to them the following day, perhaps because it was when he
was due to meet the Angel Jibrīl 鬱. However, he forgot to
say 'God willing'.[45] Days went by and the Pagans began to
revel in this, believing that they had finally overcome this
man and disproved his previous claims. It is reported that
after 15 days divine revelation came, bringing verses from
chapters Al-Kahf and Al-Isrā, not only responding to the
questions in much detail but also teaching the Prophet of
God 鬱 a valuable lesson. This lesson came in the form of two
verses in Al-Kahf, from which we can all learn the value of
saying '*in shā Allāh*' or 'God willing' at every juncture of life:

> "Do not say of anything 'I will do that tomorrow' without
> adding 'God willing', and remember your Lord whenever
> you forget..." (18:23–24)

---

44 The three questions were related to the People of the Cave, the rūḥ (soul), and the
righteous king who travelled to the east and west (Dhul Qarnayn).

45 Tafsīr Ibn Kathīr

Dreams Do Come True

Prophet Yūsuf ﷺ was someone who was rewarded for his patience and efforts, and his dreams certainly came true after years of belief and resilience. After welcoming his family and allowing them to settle in the land of Egypt, something significant happened which Yūsuf ﷺ was perhaps not expecting. After organising this reunion and successfully bringing his family to him, Allāh ﷻ tells us that Yūsuf ﷺ's parents,⁴⁶ as well as his eleven brothers, all bowed down in prostration to him. This is when Yūsuf ﷺ cried out: "My dear father, this is the fulfilment of that dream I had long ago! My Lord has made it come true" (12:100).

---

46 Classical commentators of the Qur'ān are divided on this issue. Some say that Yūsuf's mother had passed away, so this was his stepmother, and others say this was his aunt. See Tafsīr al-Ṭabarī for further details.

Now it all made sense—the eleven stars represented his brothers and the sun and the moon his father and mother, all prostrating to him. Decades later, what was once a young child with a dream was now a great prophet and leader seeing his dream materialise right in front of him. No one could have envisaged this; it was a story which defied all odds and one that proved dreams really can come true.

We can split dreams into two types; the first are dreams we experience during our sleep and the second are dreams we have while we're awake. Dreams whilst sleeping are a series of thoughts or images in one's head which can be influenced by various factors. This type of dream can be further divided into three categories, as our Prophet ﷺ taught us: good dreams, bad dreams and random dreams.[47]

A good dream is from Allāh ﷻ. Though not every good dream has to have a meaning, when we have a good dream during sleep, we still take it as a good sign and thank our Lord for it.

47 Sunan Ibn Mājah, Book of Dream Interpretations

A good dream is from Allāh ﷻ and is from one of the branches of prophethood. The dreams of prophets are a form of revelation and they manifest into a reality, as is what happened with Yūsuf ﷺ and as previously mentioned with Prophet Ibrāhīm ﷺ. Though not every good dream we have has to have a meaning, we still take it as a good sign and thank our Lord for this. A bad dream, we are informed, is from Satan.[48] We may wake up feeling agitated or scared, but we should seek refuge in God from this and continue as normal without looking too much into it. A random dream, on the other hand, is experienced quite frequently because it is a mishmash of different things. It may be influenced by something that has been occupying our minds or something we have been reading up on or watching. All these dreams take place whilst in the state of sleep and we generally do not have control over them.

One of the greatest visionaries ever to have lived was our Prophet ﷺ himself. He clearly had a vision for his community and wanted the best for them.

48 Ṣaḥīḥ al-Bukhārī, Book of Dream Interpretations

Our dreams are not restricted to this life, nor are they only about ourselves and our egos. They stem from our servitude to the Creator, an understanding of the greater purpose in life and our hopes for the Afterlife.

The other type of dreams are those that we do have control over and are the ones we have after we wake up. Often called a dream or a vision, they are the ability to use our wisdom and imagination to plan ahead and direct ourselves towards something great and impactful. These are the visions we should hold onto, and these should propel us towards action and striving for God's sake. The dreams that we as believers have are different to the dreams of those with no faith. Our dreams are not restricted to this life, nor are they only about ourselves or feeding our egos. Our dreams stem from our servitude to the Creator, an understanding of the greater purpose in life and our hopes for the Afterlife.

One of the greatest visionaries ever to have lived was none other than our Prophet ﷺ himself. When one of his companions was asked to describe him, he mentioned how he ﷺ was in "a constant state of worry".[49] This concern was for his *ummah* (community) and its future—such were the thoughts that occupied his mind. He clearly had a vision for his community and wanted the best for them. When it came to the Battle of the Trench, he and his companions dug for days in preparation for the campaign. However, there was one rock that the companions were not able to penetrate, so the Messenger of God ﷺ picked up the axe, invoked the name of Allāh ﷻ and struck it with all his might. This is when something astonishing happened. One third of the rock broke,

'With a vision, we have the ability to use our wisdom, and imagination, to plan, ahead and direct ourselves towards something great and impactful. 'We should hold onto these to propel us towards action, and striving for God's sake.

---

49 Al-Shamā'il Al-Muḥammadiyya, Chapter on the Speech of the Messenger of Allāh ﷺ

and he exclaimed: "God is great! I have been given the keys of Syria. By God, I can see its red palaces from where I stand!".

He struck it for a second time, breaking another third of the rock and this time announcing that he had been given the keys to Persia. He could now see its white palaces from where he stood. Upon the third strike he again praised God, shattering the remainder of the rock and giving glad tidings of the keys of Yemen.[50] With these statements, he raised the spirits of the companions by inspiring them and demonstrated his fantastic leadership qualities. These were by no means empty words, rather they were divinely inspired and summarised the great vision he had. Though the hypocrites took this as an opportunity to mock and scorn at the Muslims, little did they know that within a decade or so of this event, the world's greatest empires would collapse and this vision would undoubtedly become a reality. Thus, the questions arise: what vision do we have for ourselves and the people around us? How will we contribute and serve others through this? And most importantly, how can we make our hopes, dreams and visions a reality?

---

50 Sunan al-Nasā'ī, Book of Jihād

39

The Best of Endings

How do we measure true success when evaluating our lives? Prophet Yūsuf ﷺ was the perfect example of someone who maintained a balance and achieved the best of both worlds. He was someone who gained a position of power and high social status while holding on to his faith. He not only earned the love of the people, but most importantly, he became a man most beloved to God.

Yūsuf ﷺ was fully aware of the great blessings bestowed upon him by his Lord, and the time had now come to reflect on his journey up until this point. Allāh ﷻ had taken him from the lowest point of the darkest well to a lofty position of power and influence. Allāh ﷻ had chosen him to receive divine revelation and become someone who would leave behind a lasting legacy. But as he approached the end of his life and looked back on these achievements, he knew what truly mattered to him the most. It was not the beauty he was blessed with or the authority he had or the ability to interpret dreams, it was something far more meaningful than that. Yūsuf ﷺ understood that beauty eventually fades away, power can be seized and this world would come to an end. What was important to him was the state he would be in when his time came to be taken back to Allāh ﷻ and how he would fare in the next abode. This is when he made the special *du'ā*: "My Lord! You have given me authority and taught me something about the interpretation of dreams. Creator of the heavens and the earth, You are my Protector in this world and in the Hereafter. Let me die in true devotion to You and join me with the righteous" (12:101).

Prophet Yūsuf ﷺ firstly acknowledges his worldly blessings, before proceeding to ask God for the best ending to this life and the finest outcome in the life to come. Imagine, one of God's prophets, the best of all people, is beseeching Him to be taken in a state of submission and devotion to Him! In other words, he is asking Allāh ﷻ to die as a Muslim. This is the concern that Yūsuf ﷺ had, and this is what resonated with him the most when making this sincere supplication. The luminary companion of the Prophet ﷺ, Abū Bakr al-Ṣiddīq ﷺ, used to also ask Allāh ﷻ to let the best of his lifetime be its ending and the best of his deeds to be the one he seals his life with.[51] As we know, Abū Bakr ﷺ passed away at the same age as the Prophet ﷺ did, was buried next to him ﷺ and is someone who

---

51 Muṣannaf Ibn Abī Shaybah, Book of Supplications

the Qur'ān refers to as the "Ṣāḥib" (Companion) of the Prophet[52]—a distinguished title earned only by him. Thus, it was a common practice of the righteous to ask for a blessed ending and to die in a state in which God is pleased with them and they are pleased with Him.

The final part of the *du'ā* that Prophet Yūsuf ﷺ made was to ask Allāh ﷻ to join him with the righteous in the next life. Some of the commentators mention that he was specifically asking to be in the company of his forefathers Ibrāhīm ﷺ and Ishāq ﷺ, as well as his own father Ya'qūb ﷺ—the same noble lineage that was mentioned at the beginning of this Quranic chapter.[53] However, if we take the more general meaning, we can discern that along with them, Yūsuf ﷺ wanted to be in the best of company even in the Hereafter. He wanted to be raised with the 'Ṣāliḥīn' (righteous ones), and this should also be our aim and desire. Wherever these righteous people rank in the next life, we too shall follow them if we are admitted into their company. It is famously attributed to the great Imām Al-Shāfi'ī ﷺ that he would say out of humility: "I love the righteous, but I am not of them, perhaps by their virtuous company I can attain [their] intercession." It would truly be a blessing to accompany our righteous predecessors, the revered companions, and the Messenger of Allāh ﷺ, along with the other prophets!

---

52 Qur'ān, 9:40
53 Tafsīr al-Qurṭubī

Yūsuf ﷺ understood that this world would come to an end. What was important to him was the state he would be in when his time came to be taken back to Allāh ﷻ.

Prophet Yūsuf ﷺ was an illustrious prophet who lived a blessed life. It is reported that this supplication was one of the last words he said before he departed from this world.[54] Little is known about what happened after he reunited with his family members and how long he lived for, as the Qur'ān remained silent on this. However, what we do know is that this was the beginning of a new era. His father, Prophet Ya'qūb ﷺ, had the famous title of 'Isrā'īl', thus his sons became known as Banī Isrā'īl (the Israelites). The Israelites settled in Egypt, each forming their own clan and becoming a people who were favoured by God. The next generation of prophets and messengers would soon emerge from this family, making way for the likes of Sulaymān ﷺ, Mūsā ﷺ and 'Īsā ﷺ (Jesus). Each of these chosen servants of God continued to carry the message of our faith over the years, and all had their own story to tell. From each of their stories and experiences, we can draw a number of lessons that will help guide us in our own lives.

---

54 Tafsīr Ibn Kathīr

40

Everything Requires Reflection

With the conclusion of this enthralling story, we must follow the Quranic guidance on reflection and contemplation. We can find a plethora of stories in the Qur'ān, and though storytelling is a common feature in the Scripture, it is unlike the conventional storytelling that we may find elsewhere. Storytelling is indeed a powerful tool, particularly in an oral society like the Meccans lived in, where many of them, including the Prophet ﷺ himself, could not read or write. In the concluding verse of Sūrah Yūsuf, God explains the key reason for relating such stories: "There is certainly a lesson in the stories of such people for those who understand…" (12:111).

Here, the Arabic expression for 'lesson' is ʿibrah, which literally means to 'cross over'. Some linguists deduce that an ʿibrah is that which helps one cross over to reach a good

Quranic stories were not revealed for the purposes of mere entertainment or as a pass-time, rather the expectation always was and still is to initiate a process of reflection.

understanding.[55] One of the words for a 'teardrop' in Arabic is ʿabrah, so perhaps there is a connection between these two words. An ʿibrah is what makes you connect deeper to a story, such that it moves you to tears. No doubt, the story of Yūsuf ﷺ is one which takes us through a range of emotions and allows us to appreciate a myriad of lessons.

God commands the Prophet ﷺ to narrate these stories to the people so that "perhaps they will give thought" (7:176). The Arabic term in this verse for "giving thought" is tafakkur, which is a common expression for the act of pondering or thinking deeply about something, leading to reflective thinking. In other words, Quranic stories were not revealed for the purposes of mere entertainment or as a

---

55   Al-Rāghib Al-Asfahānī, Mufradāt al-Qurʾān

pass-time, rather the expectation was and still is to initiate a process of reflection.

Every verse in Sūrah Yūsuf as well as throughout the Qur'ān, whether related to patience, building one's character or being regular with prayers, contains guidelines and lessons which can be derived and further reflected upon. Thus, it is imperative that we take some time out to connect with these verses on a much deeper level. Our connection with the Qur'ān begins with its recitation and perhaps extends to memorisation, but it is important that we build upon that. Recitation is done with the tongue and memorisation is achieved with the mind, but reflection is accomplished with the heart. Reflection helps us to internalise the meanings of the Qur'ān, which in turn transforms us as people, enabling us to access the illuminating guidance of God's words. The heart is central to this, which is why God informs us that the "people of understanding (albāb)" (12:111) will benefit from these

Though the act of reciting the Qur'ān has immense benefits, there is nothing more powerful and nourishing than, pondering over it and bringing it into our lives.

lessons, whereas the rest of the people will overlook them. The word 'albāb' comes from the word 'lubb' in Arabic, which is perhaps the core of our heart—that which gives us reason and understanding.[56]

After reading and briefly studying a Quranic chapter like Sūrah Yūsuf, we should ask ourselves so many questions as part of our own reflection process. Have I truly understood what it means to be patient? How can I infuse optimism into my own life? How do I react in moments of difficulty? What can I do to rid my heart of envy? What other lessons can I take from my reading? Each question should lead us to an action plan through which we practically implement the lessons learned. Though the act of reciting the Qur'ān has immense benefits, there is nothing more powerful and nourishing than pondering over it and bringing it into our lives. When our Prophet ﷺ was described, we are told that "his character was the Qur'ān".[57] He was a walking embodiment of it, as were his companions, and our aim should be to reach this same level through contemplation and implementation.

---

56   Tafsīr Ibn 'Āshūr
57   Al-Adab Al-Mufrad, Book on Good Character

Conclusion

The story of Prophet Yūsuf ﷺ proves to us that it is very possible to attain the best of both worlds. Here we have a man who was not only blessed with a noble lineage, undeniable beauty and an honourable position, but also someone who was bestowed with prophethood, had impeccable character and earned himself the highest of ranks in the Hereafter. This was not an easy feat but was earned with much struggle, coming after a series of difficult trials. To achieve what he did required pure faith in God, steadfastness and, of course, a beautiful patience.

Just imagine what our Prophet ﷺ would have felt when reflecting upon this chapter during one of the most difficult periods of his life. After losing his wife Khadījah ﷺ and his uncle Abū Ṭālib, further abuse and extreme hostility rapidly followed from his own people and from the people of Ṭāʾif. He realised that he was no longer safe, even in Makkah, and that his days were now numbered there. Thus, Sūrah Yūsuf would have played a huge role in overcoming this as it was one of the more recent revelations he was gifted with. The story of Yūsuf ﷺ is one which, as we have seen, highlights very similar struggles. This chapter covers how Yūsuf ﷺ dealt with loss and trauma, how his relationship with his own family members turned toxic and how he had to leave his hometown for a foreign land. It taught our Prophet ﷺ how those before him had also experienced adversity, how they shone in moments of darkness and showed mercy in unprecedented situations. This revelation must have given him such relief and clarity, which would then be related to his companions, who would also feel the same way for they too were struggling and floundering.

Such is the beauty of this story, which more than 1,400 years later we still relate to and reflect upon. Though we now find ourselves in a completely different location and era, we still experience the same struggles mentally, physically and spiritually. We may not be stuck in a well, but we are most likely enveloped by some other darkness. We may not be in a cell, but we have perhaps been imprisoned by our fears or worries. We may not have had our shirts torn, but our hearts certainly have been. One thing that is the same, however, is that we all have faith, and although our faith can fluctuate depending on the circumstances, we must hold on to it no matter what.

Faith is what Prophet Nūḥ ﷺ had when he embarked on the boat with a handful of believers and said: "In the name of Allāh it shall sail and anchor".[58] Faith is what Prophet Ibrāhīm ﷺ had before he was flung into the fire and said: "Allāh is sufficient for me".[59] Faith is what Prophet Mūsā ﷺ

---

58 Qurʾān, 11:41
59 Ṣaḥīḥ al-Bukhārī, Book of Tafsīr

had before he split the sea, paving the way for his people, and said: "No, my Lord is with me! He will guide me".[60] And faith is undoubtedly what Prophet Muḥammad ﷺ had as he hid in the cave with Abū Bakr ؓ and said: "Do not grieve! Allāh is with us".[61] It is our faith in the Almighty that should carry us through the uncertainty and turmoil in our lives. Just like Prophet Nūḥ ﷺ still had to build the boat, and Prophet Mūsā ﷺ still had to strike the sea with his staff, and Prophet Yūsuf ﷺ still had to meticulously plan to successfully reunite his family, we too must do whatever we can while remaining firm in our faith.

The Qur'ān is an endless ocean, and this chapter along with all its lessons, are but a drop of water compared to the vastness that we have access to. There are many pearls yet to be discovered by us, and so our aim should be to continuously search for them by reciting and reflecting over its verses. With the conclusion of one journey is the beginning of another, and just like Prophet Yūsuf ﷺ never stopped believing and Prophet Yaʿqūb ﷺ never stopped hoping, we should endeavour to never stop learning and investing in ourselves. May Allāh Almighty grant us a beautiful patience on each of our journeys and bless us with the best outcome in this life and the next!

---

60 Qur'ān, 26:62
61 Qur'ān, 9:40

Have faith in Allāh ﷻ,
exercise beautiful patience
and express gratitude for
the ability to go and grow
through life's hardships,
for the tree that is rooted
in gratitude will only bear
fruits of positivity.

⇛⇛ Selected Bibliography ⇚⇚

Qur'ān Translations:

Abdel Haleem, M.A.S. (2004) *The Quran: A New Translation*, Oxford University Press

Khattab, M. (2016) *The Clear Quran*, Book of Signs Foundation

Tafsīr Works:

Rāzī, F. (2005) *Tafsīr al-Rāzī*, Beirūt: Dār al-Fikr

Ibn Kathīr, I. and Mahdī (2011) *Tafsīr al-Qur'ān al-ʿaẓīm*, Beirūt: Dār al-Kitāb al-ʿArabī

Al-Ṭabarī, I. J. (2001) *Jāmiʿ al-Bayān fī Ta'wīl Āy al-Qur'ān*, Dār Hujar.

Ibn ʿĀshūr, M. (1984) *Tafsīr al-Taḥrīr wa-al-tanwīr*, Tūnis: Dār al-Tūnisīyah lil-Nashr

Al-Qurṭubī, M. (2006) *Al-Jāmiʿ li Aḥkām al-Qur'ān wa 'l-Mubayyin limā Taḍammanathu min al-Sunnah wa Āy al-Furqān*, Beirut: Resalah Publishers

Ḥadīth Works:

Salahi, A. (2018) *Al-Adab al-Mufrad: A Perfect Code of Manners and Morality*, The Islamic Foundation, UK

Al-Naysābūrī, M. (2010) *Ṣaḥīḥ Muslim*, Damascus: Dār al-Fayḥā'

Al-Bukhari, M.I. (1979) *Ṣaḥīḥ al-Bukhārī* (vol. 1-6), Kazi Publications, Lahore, Pakistan

Other Works:

Al-Iskandarī, I.A. (2014) *The Book of Wisdoms: Kitāb al-Ḥikam, A Collection of Sufi Aphorisms*, White Thread Press

Al-Aṣfahānī, R. (2014) *Al-Mufradāt fī Gharīb al-Qur'ān*, 7 ed. Beirut: Dār al-Maʿrifah

Mubarakpuri, S.R. (2011) *The Sealed Nectar*, Darussalam

Notes

Made in the USA
Monee, IL
17 February 2024